HOWARD ON HOWARD

"I've had the same concept from the beginning. I'd watch my dad commute. When he was stuck in the car, he'd just sit and listen to the news. And I thought, 'Wouldn't it be great if he was laughing?' If every once in awhile he heard a disc jockey say something funny, something that made him glad he was there?

"Whenever I ran into bosses who tried telling me my kind of show wouldn't work, I always thought about that one miserable bastard on the parkway in his car. And I just knew if I could make him happy, then I'd be all the rage."

Howard Stern,
Rolling Stone Interview

HOWARD STERN:
BIG MOUTH

Jeff Menell

PINNACLE BOOKS
WINDSOR PUBLISHING CORP.

PINNACLE BOOKS are published by

Windsor Publishing Corp.
475 Park Avenue South
New York, NY 10016

Pinnacle and the P logo are trademarks of Windsor Publishing Corp.

First Printing: September, 1993

Printed in the United States of America

Dedication

This book is dedicated to my beautiful wife Lisa, who kept our beautiful newborn daughter Dara out of my hair while I wrote this book.

Acknowledgments

I am deeply indebted to my friends/agents/wardens Scott and Barbara Siegel, who not only got me into this mess but stayed there with me until the end. I thank them for their warmth, laughter, guidance, and some Yiddish terms thrown my way.

I'd also like to bestow a warm thank you on my "nice guy" editor Paul Dinas, whose infectious enthusiasm helped keep me focused throughout. He got me through some rough spots.

Many thanks to my friend and mentor David Hajdu for all of the work, tips du jour, care, and friendship heaped on me over the years.

And of course the biggest thank you goes to my wife, Lisa, for her love, understanding, constructive criticism, joint eating binges, did I mention understanding, and for being my best audience.

I'd also like to thank all the people mentioned in the book who were willing to talk on the record, as well as Simon Nathan, Cynthia Mangoes, and all of the other helpful people who shared their wealth of knowledge with me. A big thanks to Scott and Scott's friend Mike.

And now, finally, I must thank Howard Stern. He did not help at all in the completion of this book, but I just want to thank him for all the laughs and smiles over the years. If not for him, I wouldn't have written this book. Thanks, King.

CHRISTE
GROONROOS
GRONROOS

Introduction

This morning while in the shower I was listening to Howard, as always. In the short time it took me to cleanse my sweaty body, Howard made fun of Regis Philbin, discussed his upcoming apology to the Mayor of Dallas, complained about New Line Cinema who was supposed to produce (and still might) Howard's *The Adventures of Fartman,* bitched about his sister Ellen and her constant comparing of Howard to her husband — and that's just while I was shampooing my hair.

Yes, I am a Howard Stern fan, and I'm proud. It wasn't always this way for Howard fans. If you think gays had to stay in the closet, not too many years ago being a Howard fan had an even worse stigma attached to it. "What?! You like that jerk? What's wrong with you?" It just wasn't worth it.

Today, Howard is more popular than ever, and it's actually cool to like him. For us die-hard, longtime Howard nuts, this is in fact sort of disappointing. It's like when you discover an unknown restaurant where the food is out of this world, very few people know about it, and you receive preferential treatment. Then some idiot, probably the restaurant's owner, spreads the word and you can't get a reservation for a year. No one cares that you were among the pioneers.

One good thing about Howard's growing fame is that it lengthens his longevity, which is something we all care about. Life without Howard seems inconceivable, and in all honesty, at this point, it seems unlikely as well. Besides his radio show, which is currently broadcast into fifteen cities, Howard has his unique "interview" show on the E!-Entertainment Channel, and he may or may not still have his two-picture deal with New Line Cinema. He's hot, he's Howard.

As any true Stern fan can tell you, there is no better way (other than sexual) to wake up than to be startled out of a dream and find one's self in the middle of Boy Gary being bawled out by Howard. Poor Boy Gary. Yet is there any among us that wouldn't give anything to be in his place? I mean, how fun would that be, to be a part of that crazy group? Can you even imagine loving a job as much as that one? I can, and have, many times. It is this Howard envy that partly makes each of us a fan.

How many times have you seen something on TV, whether it is on the news, some awards program, or seeing Chelsea Clinton at the Presidential Inaugural celebration, and thought, "Oh, man. I can't wait to hear what Howard will say about that tomorrow?" For us millions of Stern fans, Howard invades our lives even when he's not on the airways.

It's true that Howard, at times, can be insensitive, raunchy, cruel, disrespectful, and even pompous. But the bottom line is that he *is* funny. I mean really funny. Consistently funny. This, more than anything else, not even his outrageousness, is what makes Howard truly the King of all Media.

His targets are limitless, ranging from the common masses to superstars. Women, gays, blacks, Filipinos, Jews, Latinos, Roseanne and Tom Arnold, Larry King, Don Imus, Los Angeles morning deejays Mark Thompson and Brian Phelps, former and current employers, even sponsors. No one is safe from Howard's ire nor can hide from his unerring aim.

Some critics try to label Howard as an inciting bigot when he says something disparaging against the blacks or the Jews, and the fact that he's Jewish and Robin is black is just a convenient facade to hide behind. But I believe that Howard says many of the things he does to: one, get laughs; two, have something interesting to talk about; three, stir up a little controversy. He may deny it, but when the FCC fined Howard's parent company, Infinity Broadcasting, it was the best gift he could have hoped for. Any listener of Howard knows how much air time Howard has gotten from the FCC business. It has made him the First Amendment Poster Boy, and he loves it. Anything that shines the limelight on our fair-haired, long-haired boy, he embraces with welcoming arms.

Howard says the things, and asks the questions, that we like to hear. He's got big balls, even if he does have a small penis (his claim, not mine). He has an everyman appeal that latches onto the lowest common denominator in most of us. But besides carrying on about things that we can relate to, he does so in a comically ranting style that is refreshing, and, once again, funny.

And if nothing else, Howard Stern is true to himself above all. Even though he needs us fans to propel him to the level of stardom he is so hungry for, basically he views us with disdain. He berates us, belittles us, questions our collective intelligence, hangs up on us—and we keep coming back for more, begging for it in fact. This is the incredible phenomenon of Howard Stern. In spite of all his no-talent impersonators, there is no one like him. He is the King, and long may he live.

One

Born to Be Wild

By no means can Howard Stern be considered an overnight success. Howard was born January 12, 1954, and in 1976, at twenty-two, Howard took his first paying job at WRNW-FM in Briarcliff, New York. Then fate sent him to WCCC in Hartford, Connecticut, where he first met wild man Fred Norris. Steadfastly avoiding job longevity, Howard picked up in 1980, and became the morning man at WWWW-FM in Detroit, until, of course, they switched to a country music format. Commenting in a *New York* magazine article as to why this forced him to leave, Howard explained, "I have no tolerance for country music. I mean, the Judds (then still a duo) remind me of Nazi women. I feel they could kill me."

From there, in 1981, he went to WWDC-FM in our nation's capital, where, Howard introduced "raunch radio" to our nation's airwaves. It's also noteworthy because that is where Howard met Robin Quivers, a former Air Force nurse who was the station's newswoman. They hit it off right away, and their on-air banter became so popular that Howard was allowed to add Fred to the show, who in turn added a number of memorable characters to the program, including God, who delivered the daily weather report. In a Richard Nixon-like voice, "God" would say things like, "Tonight I think I'll make it rain, Howard."

In less than two years, Howard more than tripled the station's morning drive audience. One of the now legendary stories about Howard was that after Air Florida Flight 90 tragically plunged into the Potomac River, Howard tried calling the airline to ask what the one-way fare was from National Airport to the Fourteenth Street Bridge. But according to Howard, in a *People* magazine article, it was outrage and not insensitivity on his part that prompted his call. "I was incensed because they let a plane go up with ice on its wings," Stern explained. "People said I showed a lack of sympathy for the people who died. It was completely the opposite. Out of satire comes maybe some social action. I've done a lot worse than that in terms of tastelessness."

In similar fun phone-call fashion, after Mob hitman Big Paul Castellano was gunned down in front of Sparks Steak House in New York City, Howard called up the next day to make reservations, and then heard a dial tone after he requested to be seated in the "No Shooting" section.

What brought him in the first place to the Big Apple, his most major market to date, was a $200,000 a year offer from WNBC-AM radio. He, Alison, and daughters Emily and Debra (Ashley wasn't even a thought at the time) moved back to Long Island expecting the best.

But things weren't all that rosy for Howard. Stuck in the afternoon slot, he longed for the more desirable morning drive program, then inhabited by soon-to-be arch rival Don Imus. It wasn't long before Howard started feuding with Imus and Soupy Sales, also on WNBC at the time, and even engaged in a heated argument with then NBC station general manager John Hayes. As Howard told *Rolling Stone* magazine, "It was crazy. But it was great fucking radio."

Howard was unhappy with the way he was treated at WNBC, and the powers that be at WNBC, in spite of Howard's undeniable popularity and rating surge, were disenchanted by his questionable material and outrageousness. The qualities that, in fact, inspired them to hire the

15

one and future king in the first place.

On Monday, September 30, 1985, shortly before he was about to go on the air, WNBC fired Howard Stern. Howard's version, according to *Rolling Stone,* is "the story goes that Thornton Bradshaw, the Chairman of the Board of RCA, was riding by in his limo one day, and he turned on the station and heard me talking about doing 'Bestiality Dial-A-Date.' And I guess he didn't think it was too fucking funny."

In November 1985, after a couple of months hawking for a job via the local newspapers and television stations, Howard landed a lucrative deal with Infinity Broadcasting, where he became the afternoon guy at WXRK (K-Rock), 92.3 FM on your dial. He brought along Fred and Robin and also hired Gary Dell'Abate, whom he met at WNBC, and Jackie "the Jokeman" Martling. The crew was formed and history was about to be made. After four months Howard got the morning slot he'd been craving all along. Fate finally seemed to be dealing Howard a good hand.

In 1986, within a year after leaving, Howard's show passed WNBC in the morning ratings, and Howard and gang held a mock funeral (the first of many to come) for his competition at the Rockefeller Center offices of NBC. In the *Rolling Stone* article, Howard proudly, but mockingly, said, "Imus said if we ever beat him, he'd eat a dead dog's dick. And I was going to send him one, but I felt bad for the dog."

In August of 1986, Howard's show began simulcasting in Philadelphia on WYSP, then later on WJFK back in D.C. Today, Howard's infamous program is broadcast into at least fifteen markets, and you can be sure that's not the end of it.

In the fall of 1991, Howard's show moved into first place in the ratings, and, to celebrate, Howard held a press conference in Times Square, attracting hundreds of his crazy, freezing fans. In pure demeaning Stern fashion, which is what the crowd expected, Howard told them, "As I look at you, I see a sea of losers like me. Who would ever have thought that a sea of losers like you would make a loser like me number one?"

Having the only radio show to ever be number one in both New York and Los Angeles certainly had added confidence and security to Howard's public persona.

According to a recent Arbitron survey, more than 3.5 million people listen to Howard Stern. I'd say Howard's reign is quite secure for the time being.

Two

Da Crew

What can you say about that wild, eclectic gang of people that surrounds Howard Stern each morning? Well, the truth is: not much. The fact is that they keep pretty much to themselves.

And maybe, in some sense, it's better to believe that Robin, Fred, Jackie, Gary, and John are just who they seem to be on the show. It's even possible that they actually are.

We always hear about Howard, that he's a real nice guy off the air and much calmer. But as Howard even admitted on the air, he may tone it down a bit, but basically he's still the same person. His opinions and feelings on the people and topics he discusses on the radio don't change when he goes home.

So, one assumes it's the same for his crew. What I can tell you about Robin, most of you already know. She used to be a nurse; she has had breast reduction surgery; she's been romantically linked to Michael Swan, a soap star, as well as to Penn Jillette (of Penn and Teller); she doesn't like to talk too much about her family on the air, even when Howard tries to bring them up.

When I first started listening to this show, Robin seemed like Howard's Ed McMahon. All she did was laugh at everything he said, followed by an "Oh, Howard." I never felt she contributed to the show, other than being a foible or sounding board for Howard's antics. I even felt for awhile that maybe Howard had her around simply because she was a woman, and we all know how much Howard loves women.

Then slowly, imperceptibly, I started to appreciate Robin more and more. I came to the realization that she was a much bigger cog in this crazy wheel than I had originally given her credit for.

"Robin, let's do the news" is a phrase that each listener now longs to hear. Robin picks the top news stories of the day, reads a brief account of each, and then Howard spends minutes, sometimes longer, throwing his two million cents in. Then Robin usually reacts to Howard's reactions, and we end up with a newscast lengthy enough to be on CNN. The only difference is that Howard and Robin's newscasts make us laugh.

Bababooey, Bababooey!! Gary Dell'Abate, aka Boy Gary, aka Bababooey, aka whipping boy to Howard. Yes, we have all empathized with Boy Gary at one time or another. But who is Boy Gary? Well, according to him, he is without a doubt the most underappreciated producer in the entertainment industry.

Gary and Howard fight frequently on-air. Howard often gets pissed at Gary for abusing certain perks he had gotten because of the show, or for forgetting to do something. The specifics don't really matter. They never do when these two fight. All that matters is that Howard gets pissed, or acts pissed, but he definitely sounds pissed. And Gary, you've got to love him, *never, never, never, never* learns his lesson.

Jackie "The Jokeman" Martling. Jackie is a stand-up comic with a beer belly, the grossest toenails, an excitable personality, four jokes to his credit, and a penchant to laugh louder at his own jokes than anyone else. Apparently, Jackie's main contribution to the show is that he passes furiously written notes containing a funny line or thought to Howard during the program. Of course, Jackie isn't responsible for everything funny that comes out of Howard's mouth, but he is quick on his feet.

Fred Norris. Fred is a real mystery man. I feel he is the Dan Aykroyd/Phil Hartman of Howard's radio show. By that I mean his is the most creatively warped mind on the show. God only knows what he could come up with if he were ever really let loose.

Fred helps write all of the special bits and song parodies. He also does many impressions and characters, and is in charge of the hilarious sound effects.

Hero of the Stupid. John Melendez, otherwise known as Stuttering John, is the newest member of the crew, and I'd say the most "famous," other than Howard of course. The reason for this is John's truly amazing interviews, which have made him a "feared" man by any celebrity worth his/her salt.

I am convinced that John has the biggest balls in show business. Either that, or he really is stupid, but I don't think so. John has risked life and limb to ask some of the most outrageous questions of some truly outraged people.

Howard, Fred, and Jackie send John out with a list of questions, which John obediently asks, no matter what they are. Sometimes Howard says, "I can't believe you actually asked that!" To which the then befuddled John answers, "But it was on the list."

Stuttering John Melendez is a young, long-haired aspiring rock star who became a member of the Stern stable solely because he stuttered. His speech, though, has improved over the years he's been with the show. I guess working with Howard is a form of therapy.

But there have been times during some of his interviews when his stutter was so bad that it sounded as if his head was about to explode. This usually happens when John asks a particularly rude question or if the interviewee is bigger than he is.

He had no trouble asking Imelda Marcos, "If you pass gas at home in front of others, do you blame the family dog?" But when he asked his standard baseball player question, "Did you ever fart in the catcher's face?" of an angry Ted Williams, John really began to stammer.

In a *Rolling Stone* article on John, Howard recalled that specific moment. "When Ted Williams says to him the second time, 'What did you say?' John knows exactly what's going to happen, and he does this 'wha-wha-wha-rrr-rr-rr' and the face. He's gotten into this contortion thing now when his voice locks up on him, and his face just goes wild. He's gotten more visual."

During John's beginning days, I used to get upset when Howard made fun of John's stuttering, and felt even worse when I would laugh along. But in hindsight, this show is certainly the best thing that ever happened to John. His stutter has lessened; he now has a record contract; he's got a pretty girlfriend; he's a celebrity in his own right, and he gets to hang out with Howard.

And I have to admit, John's interviews have become my favorite moments on radio. Listening to John in action is an uncomfortable treat. Obviously, it was better on television where you could see the incredulous reactions of John's victims.

It was always nice to see some big star laugh good-naturedly at John's obvious attempt to shock. Yet, at the same time, it was hard to blame any of these people for getting mad at John's sometimes vicious verbal assault. I mean, the questions he asked could just blow you away. Here's a mere sampling:

* To Gennifer Flowers, the woman who allegedly had an affair with then candidate Bill Clinton: "Gennifer, did the governor wear a condom?" and "Do you plan to sleep with any other Presidential candidates?"
* To baseball great Carl Yastrzemski: "Who do you think took more balls in the chin, Yogi Berra or Rock Hudson?"
* To Marsha Mason: "What did Neil Simon look like naked?"
* To Chevy Chase: "How long do you think it will be before Dan Aykroyd explodes?"
* To Anthony Quinn: "Which would you prefer, to have someone pick your nose or suck your ear-

wax out with a straw?" The charming Mr. Quinn's reply: "Both very unpleasant."

* To the Dalai Lama: "What's it like to wake up in the morning and realize you're God?" and "Do people come up to you on the street and say, 'Hello, Dalai'?"

* To Liz Smith: "Why are you such a fat cow?"

* To Walter Mondale: "Did you ever worry that (Geraldine) Ferraro would get cramps in office?"

* To a bulimic Ally Sheedy: "Did you puke today?"

* To Reggie Jackson he asked the same fart question he asked Ted Williams, but Reggie answered: "Sure, and if you hang out long enough, I'll fart in *your* face."

* To Ringo Starr: "What did you do with the money?"

Ringo: "What money?"

John: "The money your mother gave you for singing lessons."

Ringo: "I spent it on fish and chips."

Yes, we cringe in awe as John hounds these unsuspecting celebrities. But now with fame, comes the problem of recognition. Many people now know who John is and what he looks like. According to the *Rolling Stone* piece, in order to sneak into a Friars Club roast for Chevy Chase, John actually put on a suit and donned a fake mustache. Oh, the things he'll do to get the interview!

Certainly, John has his own favorite, or at least most memorable, moments. "The hardest one," John told *Rolling Stone*, "was Fred Gwynne. I had to promise this girl, this beautiful publicist, that I wouldn't ask him anything about 'The Munsters.' I said, 'Hey, don't worry; this is going to be a piece about his work in the theater,' and she's right next to me, right, when I ask him if he signs his pictures 'Fred Gwynne' or 'Herman Munster.' She's there and you could see her just. . . . That's why I stutter so much."

I remember that particular interview. Fred Gwynne was actually, I thought, quite a good sport. Although you could hear in his voice that he was keeping his temper in check. I believe when John asked him the above question, Mr. Gwynne replied, "John, I'm going to pretend you didn't ask that." It was a classy and effective response. All I know is that Howard and the gang were in hysterics when they played this back in the studio.

John is insulated with either a youthful naivety or ignorance. But to him, he can't see what the big deal is about asking these questions. Continuing in the *Rolling Stone* piece, John explains, "I'm not an insensitive guy, you know. I think it's all in good fun. People get all uptight about it. I think it's ridiculous because, I mean, if a celebrity can't deal with being asked what kind of reading material they read while on the bowl it puts them in a true light, out of their character."

Once on the Channel 9 TV show Howard said about John, "There is no show on television that would give an animal like this a job interviewing people for a living! Look at him! What a mess!" Even the National Stuttering Project got on Howard's case about his making fun of John's stuttering (although their spokesman, Ira Zimmerman, later became a big Stern fan).

"John stutters," says Howard in the *Rolling Stone* piece. "What am I going to do, hide it? Tell him not to do interviews? John has a very successful career out of it. And I disagree that we make fun of John just because he stutters. We make fun of John because he's wacky. I'm sure there are plenty of stutterers who couldn't do what John does."

John agrees. "People always ask me, 'Howard treats you so bad, how do you deal with it?' But Howard doesn't just make fun of me, he makes fun of everyone. I got a letter from a stutterer who said, 'Thank you so much. Thanks to you, when I go out, if I start stuttering, people just say, "Oh, you stutter like Stuttering John." ' And the thing is, it breaks the stigma, it breaks the wall . . ."

In fact, none of the teasing seems to bother John, except for one thing. It's okay when Fred does his dead-on impression of John, but for some reason John goes absolutely berserk when Leslie West imitates him. If you really want to hear John stutter, just get him started on Leslie.

Howard has said that if John stops stuttering, he's off the show, but John doesn't believe it. Howard, though, insists, "Oh yes, he'd absolutely be out of a job. He wouldn't be that funny anymore. If we fail to write him a funny question, the stutter actually delivers the home run. We encourage his stuttering. In fact, I believe his stuttering has gotten worse since he's been with us. I think I make him nervous."

Along with the rewards that come with John's newfound fame, there are also some repercussions. Back in 1990, John went to a party for Grace Jones at Stringfellows, a club in New York City. While there he interviewed Rock Hudson's former lover Marc Christian, as well as others. Then things started to turn strange.

According to the *New York Post*'s Page Six, John then hit on a woman even though she was with another guy. She said John "was trying to pick me up. He wouldn't go away. He was hot for me. He wasn't even my type. I like muscular guys. He looked like a hippie."

Apparently, John got the surprise of his life when he learned that she used to be a man. A journalist who witnessed the whole thing told the

Post, "He definitely freaked out. I told him, 'She's more of a man than you'll ever be and more of a woman than you'll ever get.' "

Anyway, John's version, as one would suspect, is a bit different. He told the *Post* he didn't even meet the woman until he got into a limousine to go to another club. "I looked around and I saw that someone in the car had a tape recorder and it was on. I said, 'This is a setup.' I swear to God on a stack of Bibles, I didn't even touch her—I mean him." He does admit that she was pretty but says that he knew all along she was a guy. According to another *Post* source, "Every woman he met afterwards he'd ask, 'Are you a transsexual?' He insulted a lot of women."

I remember John defending himself in a frenzied fashion on Howard's show after Howard brought up the nasty affair. John's reasoning for this setup is that the people at the party must have thought he was a homophobe, based on the leading questions he was asking Marc Christian and others.

Just another colorful story in the growing Stuttering John legend. Forget the other videos like "Butt Bongo Fiesta," Howard should put together a compilation video of John's unforgettable interviews.

Three

Howard's Women

Alison Stern. Mother of Howard's three children and wife *extraordinaire*. The very least you can say about Mrs. Stern is that she is an amazingly good sport. She has had to put up with a lot from her on-air husband over the years, and, naturally, sometimes she gets mad. Mostly, however, she takes it all with the dash of salted humor with which Howard spices things up.

There was one time, though, where Howard crossed even his wife's liberal line, and he regrets it. He told *Rolling Stone* about Alison miscarrying after her first pregnancy. "I went on and joked about how I took pictures of the miscarriage from the toilet seat and sent them to the parents because they wanted pictures of their grandchildren. Alison flipped out. We had a real bad time with that." Aside from that, Howard concedes that his wife is amazingly tolerant. As true fans know, that is the understatement of the year.

Still, it must be somewhat difficult to listen to your husband spank naked girls or watch naked girls being spanked, come on to beautiful starlets claiming that his wife is dying from cancer, talk about his sexual fantasies on the air, and discuss their private sex life graphically. It makes for great radio, but sometimes one wonders about the toll it takes on their marriage. Her life is definitely not boring, especially when she calls into the program. The time she and Howard's mother were on simultaneously, and Howard edited it and called it "Dueling Yentas," was a particular treat.

Sex is a big part, but not the only part, of Howard's show.

Howard, who constantly complains about his sex life and the size of his penis, also takes pride that he has been faithful to his wife all of these years. But to tell the truth, some of his on-air antics border on infidelity. One time when he was getting a massage from a very sexy woman, he said he got aroused, and then intoned, "I think this might be cheating on my wife!"

There was one incident I remember where Howard's sexually oriented exploits got him in trouble, but it wasn't with Alison. Although I can't imagine she was overly thrilled about it.

It was Halloween 1990, and Howard, Gary, and the others (not Robin, of course) were walking through Bayside, Queens, New York. They all were wearing regular clothes and masks. Howard's mask was that of Marge Simpson. A Channel 9 TV camera crew was in tow to hopefully capture something juicy for the show. They were successful.

They went to several homes trying to gain access, but were refused. Then Susan Glickman and her friend pulled up in a car and agreed to take them back to Susan's home and give all of them a massage. Once there, Howard picked the sexy outfits he wanted the women to wear, and Howard and company stripped down and donned towels. They all got massages. Adding a weird element to things was the fact that all the men kept their disguises on throughout. According to a *New York Post* article, Gary, who was wearing a Yogi Bear mask, said, "We kept the masks on the whole time. It was like a scene from *Clockwork Orange*."

The segment aired on Howard's TV show, and it was great. But apparently that wasn't the end of it. Several months later, Mark Glickman, Susan's husband, filed a $500-million suit against Howard. Glickman, in papers filed in Manhattan Supreme Court, claims that Howard and Robin made him the object of ridicule. He claims that the King and Queen of radio made "false" statements on the air that were "full of innuendo" about him, his wife, and their marriage.

The *Post* article goes on to report that Glickman claimed that "even people who I didn't know were making terrible comments to me and about me. They were snickering at me, pointing at me, laughing at me."

According to the papers filed, Howard said that during the massage one of the crew members was standing there aroused. Later, allegedly, the crewman asked Howard, "How many times last night did you have the girl?" Howard responded, "Uh, just once." The crewman goes, "Yeah, me, too." Upset over all this, Glickman called into the radio show, and got what he should have expected. Howard told him, "Your wife is really nice. She's got a cute little body." And devil that she is, Robin added, "And she's available. Did you know that? You ought to check out how she thinks of you and the other guys in the neighborhood." Then, just to drive the nail home, Howard says, "Yeah. Although she was getting a little aroused when she was rubbing me down. Where'd you meet that horny little minx?"

Eventually, things got so bad according to Glickman that "he lived in a state of total confusion and could not concentrate on the day-to-day responsibilities of my life." The next thing he knew he was fired. Glickman's lawyer said, "Basically, what you have here is a man whose entire emotional state was destroyed by Howard Stern." Howard's lawyer retaliated, "It sounds to me on the face of it to be preposterous. This lady freely invited him into her home, and there was a TV crew there. There's no defamation here; no defamation of her husband. He may have more reason to be upset with his wife than he has to be with Howard Stern."

When my wife and I watched this Halloween treat on Howard's show, and then later learned how unhappy Mr. Glickman became, she turned to me and said, "You'd love it if I gave Howard a massage, right?" You better believe it. I know it's sick, but that's part of the Howard mystique.

Because of the lawsuit, this one incident got more press than many other similar pranks Howard pulled. And again, the question that always comes up is, "How can his wife put up with that?" It's probably easier than we realize.

In October, 1991, Glickman's suit was thrown out by the court and an appeals court later affirmed the dismissal.

One of Howard's obsessions, as most listeners know, is spanking. He's had couples come into his studio where the guy plays the drums on the woman's butt to the tune of some song. He has also had sexy little vixens lay across his lap and let him spank them, much to Howard's delighted amazement.

Back in 1988, Howard was talking about how he wanted to be spanked. One day he had some poet chick on the air. She used to do topless poetry at his live shows at a local nightspot called Club Bene. Anyway, Howard got her into a conversation about spanking. She wasn't into it, but Howard was able to convince her to give him a spanking anyway.

Listening to this broadcast at home was a major Stern fan named Donna Albanese, aka Rachel the Spanker. For some reason, the poet's lackluster effort at spanking pissed Donna off. So she wrote Howard a letter telling him that the spanking bit sucked, and then proceeded to tell him how she would go about spanking him. Howard ended up calling her.

"I was listening to the radio program when he announced he was going to call that spanking chick," Donna recalled. "Suddenly my phone rang, and I was totally flipping out. I got so excited. I just love Howard. He is so unique to me. Anyway, I answered the phone, and so as not to aggravate the King, I turned down my radio.

"He invited me to come down to the radio show for his Christmas Special. I had never spanked anyone in my life. Howard was to be my first. So I came down to the show wearing a piece of chiffon cloth tied around my hips, with no underwear on. I had on a top that showed a ton of cleavage. Amazingly, Howard didn't really seem to dig my outfit. He didn't find this particularly sexy. Apparently, he likes women to dress normally.

"The studio is set up so that Howard is facing Jackie and Fred. Then behind them is the booth where Robin lives. So I walked in, bearing an apple for Howard. I knelt down in front of him and said something like 'Annoint me with your mighty sword.'

"Back then, everyone came into the studio and stayed for the whole show. It was purer back then. Now, all of these [girls] come in to promote shows, or whatever. I'm not like that. I do things only from the heart.

"For the Christmas Show, though, everyone there was a total Howard Stern fan. I brought all of these exotic oils with me. I came there to really do a spanking, but Howard had in mind some fluff thing. That was not on my agenda at all. I said, 'Look, I didn't come down here to do this pretend thing.' I then told him to take his pants off. Then Robin got into it and said, 'Yeah, Howard. Come on. Take your pants off.' She was siding with me. Howard said, 'Well, I don't want to show my bare ass to everyone in here.' So I gave him this piece of chiffon to put on after he took his pants off. I told him, 'So come on and get over my lap.' 'Come on Howard, get over her lap,' Robin piped in.

"So I got him over my lap. I think everyone

there was more amazed than I was. So I started whacking him and his ass got real red. I was just winging it. Then I was rubbing oil on his butt. Today I could do a much better job spanking him. It was a goof as opposed to when I sucked his toes which was a real turn-on.

"While I was spanking him, his mother and Alison called in. I was getting him worked up during his mother's call. Howard yelled, 'I can't control her, Mom!!!' His mother thought it was all a disgrace. I'm aggressive. Howard can't be aggressive because he has such strong morals. But I think he thinks it's okay if I do something to him.

"I was a real live wire. He liked that it was really authentic. I'm not just using Howard like these other bimbos. I told him I loved him. I could really do a better job spanking him now. I'm just more in tune to it now.

"Anyway, toe sucking was unbelievable. I was sitting under the console. The first think I did was ask him if he showered today. I had a microphone under the console with me. I wasn't wearing any underwear, so I spread my legs to give him a free shot. I was down there for an hour and a half. I was soaking wet. No one else there could really see what was going one. I was so excited. I was moaning and totally hot. I think Howard must have turned off my microphone because none of my moaning went out over the airways."

"I only wanted to go on Howard's show out of love. I never wanted to use Howard to promote anything."

So what is Howard like off the air? "Howard is kind of weird with me. One time after the U.S. Open Sores event, I was giving the crowd a bit of a show in the parking lot. I've been a nudist for twenty years so nudity is no big deal with me. So I thought I would just give the crowd a Howard Stern type of appearance. But Howard copped a bit of an attitude about it. They don't treat those *Penthouse* girls like they do me, like some sort of reject.

"This persona of his on [the] radio is an act. He really is a man of integrity, so I don't understand his attitude about what I do, since it's also only an act. I have a moral spirituality. So for Howard to judge me like that doesn't seem right. Especially since I present a lot of material for him to work off of."

Four

Some of the "Best of Stern"

I was standing in front of a building on the upper west side of New York City. It was 10:00 P.M. Although it was a nice spring night when I headed into the city, it now had turned cold, windy, and ominous.

At 10:05 P.M. I started to wonder if I had the wrong address, it being my nature to doubt myself. Suddenly a car pulled up in front of me, honked its horn, and a person I had never met before beckoned me into his car.

"Jeff?" he said.

"Scott?" I said.

Neither of us, I now realize, had answered, but we each assumed the other to be the person we were each supposed to meet that evening.

"You got the tapes?" I asked.

"Yup," he responded for the first time that evening.

"You got the portable?"

I nodded assent, realized we were in sync, and began to relax for the first time since I left my wife, child, and dog in our cozy home.

Scott is what you would call a major Howard Stern fan, even though he no longer has the opportunity to listen to him every morning. But back when Howard was on WNBC, Scott used to tape Howard's best bits, and to date has in the neighborhood of one hundred audio tapes loaded with classic Howard and company. It is to my good fortune that Scott answered my ad in *The Village Voice,* and offered to let me listen to these valuable tapes, with him as my knowledgeable guide.

With the aid of his good-natured friend Mike, and Mike's apartment, the three of us spent the next six hours overcome by Howardmania. Listening to Howard late at night is a very different experience than listening to him in his natural habitat of the morning hours. For me personally, it was also a treat because I had never listened to Howard when he was on WNBC. The show was different back then, and, ironically, the same. It's a curious thing. Howard still seems so outrageous today, but he seemed to have more of a desperate energy back then. He probably felt the need to try harder, and that he did, with nonstop bit after bit, tirades against something or someone, and the always present clapping and laughter in the background. Most of this is still present in Howard's radio program today, but in comparison it seems a bit more subdued, and perhaps more confident as well, than it did during his WNBC stint.

Scott has called into many shows, including Howard's, Richard Bey's, Tom Snyder's, Larry King's, and others. He is also a bit of a celebrity himself, having had a nationally televised moment with then candidate Bill Clinton. At that particular rally, Scott, while surrounded by Secret Service men, confronted Clinton and tried to get him to call Bush a racist because of Bush's membership to some exclusive club. Clinton chose not to get into name calling, and Scott ripped up his Clinton sign right in front of the soon-to-be-President.

Anyway, the morning after the event, a sleeping Scott was awakened by his friend Mike (yes, the one with the apartment), who excitedly told him that Howard was talking about Scott at that moment. Scott immediately called Boy Gary, and Gary dutifully put Scott on the air with Howard. Scott lasted a good ten minutes with Howard, which — as any Howard fan knows — qualifies as a booming success.

But enough about Scott. In the six hours spent

that evening, we only touched upon the tip of the Howard iceberg. And though it may have only led to a few paragraphs in this book, for me it was a terribly fun evening spent laughing in the comfortable company of two other Howard Stern fans.

For those fans who have been with Howard since the beginning, just the names of the following bits are enough to elicit warm smiles and an occasional belly laugh. For myself who never heard these classic bits, just fill in the blanks with your knowledge of Howard and his crew, and you'll get the idea. Of course, reading Howard is nowhere near the same as listening to him. But if you just use your imagination you could easily hear Howard, Robin, Fred, and the rest of the crazy gang. Besides, as Howard's "favorite" DJ Cousin Brucie always said, "Radio is theater of the mind."

Some were lewd, some were crass, some were controversial, but all, to varying degrees, were, and still are, funny. Here is but a mere sampling, in no particular order, of Howard's comic wares over the years:

* The often mocked Mister Rogers takes another hit in "Mister Nixon's Neighborhood," wherein the former Commander-in-Chief has a dog named Herpes ("because he won't heal") and a pain-in-the-ass son-in-law married to his

daughter Julie who can magically make butter from a butterfly and horseradish from a horsefly. Mr. Nixon eagerly awaits to see what young David Eisenhower can make from a pussy willow.

* In another visit to the neighborhood, we find Mister Nixon playing the sick game, "Find Mr. Elephant's Trunk" with the local children.

* In the 1984 bit (which predates the current controversial gays in the military issue) "Homo Pyle, USMC," Homo is looking for a few good men, finds that it's hard to move fast in cha cha heels, and also that no one wants to serve guard duty with him. "Would you pick up my rifle, please?"

* Continuing with this theme, in "Tennis Without Balls," we find a tough-sounding Martina Navratilova hitting on the demure Chris Evert. "Stick with me kid and you'll get all the beaver you want." Asked about her chances in the upcoming tournament, Martina responds, "I can lick all those broads."

* In "The Lost Alice and Trixie episode of the Honeymooners," Ralph threatens to send Alice to the moon after finding her in bed with Mrs. Norton. "Trixie already took care of that, Ralph," Alice says.

* Howard plays Gene Rayburn, Jr., in his own version of "The Match Game." Gene queries Mr. Haney about Zsa Zsa Gabor (even though it was Eva who starred in "Green Acres"), and the mulish Haney observes, "If Zsa Zsa has one more face lift they'll be calling her the bearded lady." The rest of the panel includes Ann Landers and Lou Ferrigno, both of whom are mercilessly made fun of, and the where-is-he-now Richard Dawson. In response to the phrase (*blank*) cabin, Lou guesses incorrectly, "Menachem Cabin?"

* Now one of my favorite bits, and one which I wish they'd bring back, is "Stump the Jokeman" featuring Mrs. Flemstein (Fred Norris). The jokes Mrs. Flemstein tells are all stereotypical in nature, but it is Fred's voice and delivery that make this such a fun bit. Besides, as we all know, no subject, or race, is off limits to Howard and company. Jokes like:

How did Helen Keller discover masturbation? Trying to read her own lips.

Why did the Polish guy stick ice cubes up his nose? To keep his lunch cold.

How do we know Adam and Eve weren't black? Ever try to take a rib away from a black man?

Why do Polish babies have big heads? So

they don't fall out when their mamas are dancing the Polka.

* And let's not forget the Indian comic "Morty Gandhi," and his famous relatives: Gandhi of Mayberry, Amos and Gandhi, and Gandhi Williams.

* Another "Lost Honeymooners" episode turned up, this one being the "Black Neighbors" episode, where the black Washington family moves in next door and Ralph tells Alice to pack the bags. A surprisingly upset Norton tells the Washingtons to turn down their damn jungle music or he'll steal their watermelons.

* And of course there are the famous, and infamous, Dial-A-Dates: Gay Dial-A-Date, Lesbian Dial-A-Date, Dwarf Dial-A-Date, Hooker Dial-A-Date, Dominatrix Dial-A-Date, and unnaturally, Bestiality Dial-A-Date. In these bits, Howard would arrange for a guest from one of these groups and encourage callers to answer questions in the hope of winning a date.

* "The Cancer Man" was a particularly cruel parody about the late Sammy Davis, Jr.'s bout with throat cancer. Singing to the tune of "Candy Man," Howard, as Sammy, belts out hysterically crude lyrics about his illness.

After this bit, according to *People* magazine, Fred said off the air, "We've hit a new low. It's like we're telling people, 'Go ahead, we dare you to listen.' " A smiling Howard, meanwhile, suggested they play the tune a few more times.

* And we haven't heard "Out-of-the-Closet-Stern" for quite a while. This is the bit where a gay-sounding Howard and Mr. Blackswell call "stars" we haven't seen or heard from in a long time, such as Gordon Jump ("WKRP in Cincinnati"), Rerun (from "What's Happenin'?"), Dave Madden ("The Partridge Family"), and many other where-are-they-now names.

* Both the skit "Hill Street Jews" and song "Hymie Town, Hymie Town," not too surprisingly, upset some of Howard's Jewish listeners.

* And The Magic Johnson song really ticked off Howard's Los Angeles listeners, where Magic is even more godlike than Stern. The lyrics poke fun at Johnson's sex life and his HIV positive status.

* It's hard to forget "Not for Goyim Only," where Rabbi Murray Kahane of the Temple B'Nai Vegas in Atlantic City, visiting with his lovely wife Bernice, performs "Purple Haze" in Yiddish.

* One of my personal favorites is Fred Norris playing Kurt Waldheim, Jr., doing "Who's the Jew?" where he gives a listener three famous names, and he or she has to guess who's really Jewish. It is both insulting and informative. And it's obvious that Fred has a lot of fun with it.

* When Howard heard about a judge named Israel Rubin, he said the guy might as well call himself Jewy Jew.

* In "A Hebrew Proposal," a take-off on the recent Redford film, "Indecent Proposal" an impersonated Woody Allen tries to get Robin for a million dollars. You see, it all started when the station manager, Tom, informed Howard and Robin that the FCC has fined them $1 million. Meanwhile, Woody has been watching Robin on the TV game show "Scattergories." Robin, out of desperation, takes Woody's offer. He is in the process of charming her with hilarious lines when Howard miraculously saves the day by selling Gary's teeth to a piano company.

* "Gaystoke: The Legend of Tarzan, Lord of the Gay Apes" — is pretty much self-explanatory.

* "Buttman — The Movie" a parody of "Batman" — when The Poker calls up, butler Alfred tells him, he can't hear his voice very well because

there are some dingleberries caught in the receiver.

* "Mr. Ed Meets Jessica Hahn"—a funny match made in hell.

* "The Ben Stern Day-Care Center"—When Howard was about seven years old, he and his sister, Ellen, went with their father, a recording technician, to his studio, where Dad taped a session of him asking them difficult questions and then berating them (Howard, in particular) when they answered like the children that they were. Howard took excerpts of that old tape and created a weirdly funny day-care session.

* "Phony Phone Calls"—Howard has done dozens of these, many times it is just a prelude to telling a listener that he or she has won some sort of prize. One of the best was when Howard called a school principal, who just won a K-Rock vacation, and pretended to be a father of a Tourette Syndrome son. Fred, pretending to be the thirteen-year-old son, would scream wild epithets in the background, while the principal miraculously maintained his composure.

* Fred the Elephant Boy as the Ghost of Speech Impediment Past and Quinton the Stutterer as Scrooge in *A Christmas Carol*. These two

personalities were listeners whom Howard brought into the show to the strange delight of millions.

* "Mayberry, R.F.D. — Twenty-Five Years Later" — "Whoever would have thought that me, Floyd the barber, would become the biggest cocaine dealer in North Carolina?"

* Then, there's the classic fake phone call of them all, "The Elephant Man Phone Call." After Michael Jackson was reported to have tried to buy the Elephant Man remains, Howard decided to give it a try himself. He called the London hospital in control of the remains and talks to a very proper woman. She was the ultimate straight person to Howard's outrageous clowning. She hung up on him eventually, because Howard was laughing so hard.

* There is one more that is also a personal favorite of mine. It's when Howard had June Foray, the voice of Rocky the Squirrel, in the studio, along with football legend Dick Butkus, and Howard convinced this sweet woman to do a skit about Rocky getting a woody. It was hilarious, and I thought Dick Butkus was going to hemorrhage from laughing so hard. But after playing the bit several times, June Foray told Howard she was upset at having done it and asked him po-

litely if he would refrain from airing it again. To Howard's credit, and our chagrin, he agreed. So this one won't even air on the reruns of past shows known as the "Best of Stern." In keeping with June Foray's wishes, and living up to Howard's honorable standards, I, too, refuse to go into the details of the bit.

Of course, there are many more, not to mention more to come. But we all have our personal favorites, and these are mine. Sorry, if I've left out some of your favorites.

Five
Howard's Hot Seat

What do Donald Trump, Arnold Schwarzenegger, and Sting have in common? Not much—except, of course, for the money thing. Then there's Howard. These three, and many other surprising figures in entertainment, sports, and politics, have guested on Howard's radio and TV shows.

Who has he had on? Jerry Seinfeld, David Brenner, David Letterman, Demi Moore, Sylvester Stallone, Frank Stallone, Jackie Stallone, Pat Cooper, Andrew Dice Clay, Alec Baldwin (But no Kim Basinger, damn it!), Stephen Baldwin, Chevy Chase, Bob Hope, Whoopi Goldberg, Joe Walsh, Leslie West, Bon Jovi, Robert Blake, Corey Feldman, Corey Haim, Linda Blair, Sally Kirkland, Sally Kellerman, Steve Guttenberg, Rob Lowe,

Melissa Gilbert-Brinkman, Richard Belzer, Gilbert Gottfried, Luke Perry, Sandra Bernhard, Martha Raye's husband, Dick Cavett, Gene Siskel and Roger Ebert, Ed Koch, Al Sharpton, Don King, Senator Alfonse D'Amato, Milton Berle, Joan Rivers, Dick Clark, Jessica Hahn, Geraldo Rivera, Suzanne Vega, Zsa Zsa Gabor, Dr. Joyce Brothers, Dr. Ruth Westheimer, Al Roker, Len Berman, Richard Harris, Bobcat Goldthwait, Emo Phillips, Judy Tenuta, Curtis and Lisa Sliwa, Patty Smyth, Jay Leno, Dennis Miller, Albert Brooks, Richard Simmons, Grampa Al Lewis, Bill Boggs, Maury Povich, Robert Vaughn, Bob Denver, Dick Butkus, Dee Snyder, David Lee Roth, Mason Reese, Tom Jones, Monty Hall, Joey and Mary Jo Buttafuoco, Phoebe Snow, James Brown, Garry Shandling, Carol Alt, Ron Greschner, Keith Hernandez, Tyrone Frazier, Young M.C., Aerosmith, Penn and Teller, Leonard Marshall, Joe Clark, Papa John Phillips, Grace Slick, Max Weinberg, Nils Lofgren, Richard Marx, Al Michaels, Mario Van Peebles, Ton Loc, Milli Vanilli (or whatever they call themselves these days), Garry Marshall, Jim Belushi, Harry Shearer, Michael McKean, Bob Geldoff, Richard Pryor, Steve Rossi, Marilyn Michaels, Jimmy Breslin, George Steinbrenner, Debbie Gibson, Al Martino, George Carlin, Henny Youngman, Roger Clinton, Willie Nelson, Robert Klein, Michael J. Fox, Alice Cooper, the never-to-be-forgotten Sam Kinison, and I'm sure there's more that I've forgotten.

Not a bad list, especially considering that virtually each and every one of their appearances was memorable.

And Howard's relationships with all of these individuals certainly vary in intensity and change from day to day. As most of us know, Howard has had several on-again off-again friendships, that have resulted in some colorful feuds which always make for good radio. He has had feuds with David Brenner, Jerry Seinfeld, David Letterman, and currently is involved in a surprising feud with Richard Simmons, whom Howard now vehemently ridicules. Simmons's obsession with things named Barbie and Barbra (Streisand), as well as his affected mannerisms, make him the perfect target for Howard's zingers. He's never made clear exactly what Richard did to piss him off, but his words have been so stinging that a reconciliation seems, at this point, an impossibility. Even if you're not a Richard Simmons fan, his outbursts on Howard's show are classics.

Howard's relationships with stand-up comics seem to be the most natural. Perhaps it's because he feels he's on a level with them as far as the entertainment hierarchy goes, and also because many times they make the best guests. Kinison,

Andrew Dice Clay, Richard "the Belz" Belzer, David Brenner, and Richard Lewis are some of my favorite guests.

A great moment was when Howard decided to end the feud between Dice and Belzer. Dice had been pissed because Belzer went on national television and bad-mouthed Dice's comedy style. Dice laid into him good over the phone during a visit to Howard's show, and the two hadn't talked since. Well during this particular show, Dice was on, and Howard asked if he would stay when he brought Belzer out because Howard felt these guys should make up. It was a testy reconciliation at best, with caustic barbs being thrown all over the place, but eventually harmony was restored—thanks to Howard the peacemaker.

Howard's one-time alienation from David Brenner was the result of what sounded like an innocent remark from Howard. Apparently Howard and Robin kept asking Brenner about this young woman they saw him with at a party, and Brenner, for his own personal reasons, blew up over these "personal" questions. It truly mystified Howard and Robin. But they're all friends again. Brenner said of Howard to *Rolling Stone*, "He could get Mother Teresa to spit on him and walk off the show. He's a genius at manipulating people."

Neurotic, Johnny Cash-garbed Richard Lewis is one of my personal favorite guests and comedians. He and Howard never officially feuded, which makes him unique, but there is always an element of anger and defensiveness when Richard is on. I think he gets annoyed when Howard questions his loyalty or sincerity, but their on-air (sometimes over the phone) banter is some of the best.

Some comedians, I find, seem much funnier on Howard's radio program than they do when we see them in person or on TV. Emo Phillips and Judy Tenuta are two such people. According to Howard, these two polar opposites are secretly married (or were secretly married) though they constantly deny it. Emo's persona is that of a slow-witted child, and sometimes watching him can be a very uncomfortable experience. Then I heard him on Howard's show and found myself in hysterics. The man is quick, intelligent, and bitingly funny (even if Howard doesn't always laugh at him). Emo and Howard almost had an on-air falling-out when Howard read that Emo had said some bad things about him. Howard called Emo up and Emo spent most of the call apologizing and saying it was a typographical error.

I find Judy more outrageous than funny. What is funny is Howard's ability to get a ranting rise out of her. It doesn't take much to get Judy started. Just mention Roseanne Arnold and you can hear the steam coming out of Judy's ears. It's her unlikely association with Emo that fascinates me the most.

Another comic I enjoy more on the radio is Gilbert Gottfried. I have to admit that when I would see Gilbert on Letterman I would feel a bit weird. His squinting, persevering manner used to amaze rather than amuse me. He never seemed to care that the audience wasn't laughing. He would just keep going with the same bit, seemingly unwilling to stray from his agenda. He did, however, make me laugh quite a bit with his short, but memorable, appearances in *Beverly Hills Cop II* and both of the *Problem Child* films. He even played a "shock jock" based in part on Howard in the Andrew Dice Clay movie *Ford Fairlaine*.

But it wasn't until I first heard Gilbert on Howard's program that I really started to appreciate him. Without the distraction of his squint and mannerisms, I was able to hear his humor. His David Brenner impression hits the mark dead center, and when he and Howard do dueling Seinfelds, it's a scream. Gilbert recalls the time he and Howard called up Jerry and after they got his machine, "I imitated Jerry for about a half hour, using up all his tape. Later, Seinfeld called Howard and said 'That doesn't sound like me.' "

When Gilbert comes into the studio, sometimes unannounced, you can almost feel both him and

Howard kick into gear. It's as if they each try to top the other, but never in a mean-spirited way. It's a fun competition that each, so obviously, truly enjoys.

Gilbert's first appearance was several years ago, a booking he got while performing at Caroline's comedy club in New York City. At that time he had only heard Howard on the air once or twice, which probably explains why he wasn't apprehensive about entering the lion's den. It proved to be a smooth introduction. "It seemed like we sort of got along, as well as either me or Howard could get along with anybody."

Gilbert still doesn't listen to Howard's show all that much. "Sometimes I do. But usually when I'm not on it I try to go to sleep." When I tell Gilbert that he probably has been on the "Best of Stern" as many times as Sam Kinison, he says laughing, "Yeah, me and other dead comics. Gottfried and other dead comics."

Are any of the antics between Howard and Gottfried rehearsed? "Usually on the show nothing is planned out. It's a great atmosphere. Everybody is in there together, except for Robin who is sort of off by herself behind the glass booth. And I'm in a booth with Howard, Fred, and Jackie. I play off of Howard, or sometimes I'm in my own world. It's usually a lot of fun. I used to just stop in on the show. You know, guests would be on, and I would just like walk in on them."

So, can Gilbert tell us what Howard is like off the air? "We both act like David Niven when we're off the air."

Interesting.

Has Howard offered Gottfried a role in his upcoming film, *The Adventures of Fartman?* "Well, I've heard about it. It certainly sounds intellectual enough for me. Does he want me to do the special effects sounds?"

Gilbert says his experiences on Howard's show have all been memorable, but his timing isn't the greatest. "It's the story of my life that I always walk in when he *doesn't* have any naked girls on. One time I came in right after getting out of the hospital. I guess I felt that I was already used to the pain."

What is Fred Norris like? "It's hard to say, but I do know that I've said something *really* disgusting when I get a dirty look from Fred. That's when I get that sense of achievement, when I get that look from Fred."

From Gilbert to Jerry Seinfeld is not such a bad segue. It almost amazes me that Jerry Seinfeld, star of the phenomenally popular "Seinfeld" TV show, still does Howard's show. Not because he's so big that he doesn't *need* to do Howard's radio show, but because Howard incessantly makes fun of Jerry and puts him down. Seinfeld is a very big star these days, and yet he still calls in to the show or even drops by the studio.

On one show, Howard announced that Jerry would be dropping by. Then he got a fax from some listener who claimed that after seeing Seinfeld at a comedy club, a member of the audience asked him what he thought of Howard Stern. According to this person, Jerry said that he thought "Howard was a funny jerk and an amusing idiot." Howard immediately launched into one of his merciless attacks. And Robin, for her own reasons, jumped into the melee. Howard prayed to the Lord Jesus for Jerry to get a debilitating disease, and that his best gig will be playing Jewish weekends in the Catskills. "That he never gets another girl no matter how hard he tries. I pray that Jerry has to come in here and kiss my ass in a major way. Jesus, if you don't come through for me I'll have to go to Satan."

When Howard had the legendary Milton Berle on, he set Mr. Television up big time. It's been rumored for years that Mr. Berle is very well endowed. Anyway, Howard knew that Uncle Miltie doesn't like to discuss this particular subject. So, right before Berle was due to come out, Howard talked to about six different callers and told them he wanted all of them to ask specific questions about the size of Milton's penis once he came on the air.

So, Uncle Miltie comes on the air, he has a pleasant chat with Howard, says he'd rather not discuss the penis rumor, then agrees to talk to callers. And Howard played the innocent throughout all the penis questions. It may not be nice to play practical jokes on one of the comic pioneers, but Milton fell for it hook, line, and sinker. A proud moment for Howard, to be sure.

If you're like me, you still regret the fact that Rob Lowe never married Melissa Gilbert. These two used to be great guests, whether on together or separately. I think part of their problem began when Melissa told Howard that Rob's penis wasn't all that large. But to tell you the truth, that might have happened after they broke up for the umpteenth time. They were engaged on-and-off for a *verrry* long time.

Howard's relationship with Geraldo Rivera isn't too surprising. Not that they have too much in common. But both have lived a bit on the edge in their professional careers. Geraldo used to take on dangerous, controversial assignments when he was an investigative reporter for "20-20," and Howard is about as controversial as they gets.

These two also hit it off, I think, because of

Geraldo's willingness to let Howard ask probing questions. Geraldo may not always answer, and, on occasion, he has taken offense, but most of the time he just has fun with it.

Geraldo was gutsy, and perhaps in hindsight a bit foolish, when he agreed to fight Frank Stallone (another frequent Howard visitor) on Howard's Channel 9 TV show. This truly was an event, which gained credibility by having Michael Buffer, the well-known ring announcer, introduce the fight and terrific sportscaster Len Berman doing the blow-by-blow commentary. Naturally, the fight itself didn't live up to all the prefight hype, but Howard and the viewers loved it. And Geraldo, although losing the fight, was a great sportsman about the whole thing, as was Frank.

Geraldo appeared on Howard's E!-Channel "interview" show. In typical fashion, Howard immediately asked questions about Geraldo's alleged sexual exploits, which Geraldo had intimately detailed in his autobiography. Howard spent about ten minutes trying to understand how Geraldo could have slept with Bette Midler, then another five on Geraldo's amazing past desire to sleep with Barbara Walters. It was one of Howard's better E! shows, thanks largely to Geraldo's brashness and openness.

The relationship between Howard and Geraldo,

may be likely, but there have been a few frequent visitors to Howard's show that are quite surprising. One that still intrigues me is a guy called Donald Trump. I think "the Donald" is one of Howard's biggest coups. The surprise element aside, Mr. Trump also has turned out to be a great guest. He sometimes says things on the air that are just unbelievable coming from a multimillionaire. He has openly discussed his ending marriage with Ivana and the prenuptial contract they had (Howard strongly sides with Donald on this issue), and Marla Maples and their on-again, off-again relationship.

On Howard's E! show, Howard put up a list with pictures and names of the women that Donald has been associated with. He then went down the list, asking Donald if he had sex with each of them. And for the most part, Donald answered these personal questions. At the end, Howard did a tally, and after each face was shown on the screen, Howard said, "Had her, need her, had her, had her, need her, etc. . . ." The unflappable Donald remained unembarrassed.

Along the same lines, but not quite as unfathomable, is the friendship that has developed between Howard and Dick Cavett. Dick is a likeable intellectual with a martini-dry sense of humor. Not someone you would normally associate with

Howard Stern. Yet somehow these two hooked up about ten years ago.

"The first time I came across him was when the book *Eye on Cavett* came out," Cavett recalls. "I was out promoting the book, which was in, let me see, 1983. Now I'm sorry I looked that up. Anyway, Howard was then at WNBC, and he was on a list of book plugs I was doing. I didn't have any idea of what I was getting myself into. Howard wasn't a household name at the time, but a friend of mine had heard him a few times and gave me a slight warning that this wouldn't be a straight book interview. And it wasn't. I found it to be kind of fun.

"I was a little bit prepared, and I guess I came off alright. I wasn't a regular listener and I'm still not, although if I'm making coffee in the kitchen I'll check and see what he's up to from time to time. I've been on the radio show about as many times as I've heard it.

"The one time he called me at home apparently was a memorable one. That was the first major time I was on his current (K-Rock) show. I don't really remember it, but I'm amazed that other people still remember that particular show. And I even have a friend who quotes it as sort of a party piece. I was only sort of half awake at the time, and we matched wits, such as they are. The amazing thing is that I then had to go tape something midtown, and by the time I got made up in the

62

studio, the cabdriver and the doorman and at least three people on the crew had all told me they heard the show, and you got the impression that everyone you ran into had heard it."

It seems only fair then that Howard should have done Cavett's cable show on CNBC. "At that time I didn't have an audience in the studio, but we had put the word out and a surprising cross section, demographically, of people showed up in the Fort Lee studio. Well-dressed adults and kids showed up and we ended up having a rather large audience. It turned out Howard was a very big draw. It was a very lively and sometimes shocking show."

Dick Cavett is somewhat of an expert on comedy and comedy history, so I was understandably curious what his opinion of Howard was. "I think part of Howard's appeal is the same thing that the people who bad-mouth him don't like. That is, there are things you wouldn't dream of saying, and, if somebody else does, you would quickly label them crude or tasteless. And yet it's kind of fun to hear someone say them, especially in this age of appalling political correctness. And then you chuckle privately at something that sounds a little insulting to a minority group or grossly insulting to a human arts group. You sort of chuckle to yourself and hope that no one sees you chuckling. Howard is that bad boy. I can certainly appreciate Howard's position in the spectrum of comic art, wherever that may be.

"I think Howard is most effective on radio, for whatever reason. I do notice that if you switch on (his show) planning to listen for a minute or two, you'll find yourself caught up in it because of what is essential to his work, that sense of danger that's important in this kind of thing. That in the next moment you might just hear him go too far, so you have to keep that sense of danger there. It's sort of like the way you'll watch a near accident. Or watch traffic on a dangerous corner, feeling sort of ashamed of yourself while you're doing it."

Does he know Howard at all off the air? "Only before and after shows and during commercial breaks. He seems to be real nice, and you realize then that what he does is kind of a creative character that he goes into for the air. He's certainly not *on* in the Howard Stern public way. Once in the green room after a show we'd just done, I went up to him and said, 'Just out of curiosity, if I were to tell you something personal about myself right now, you know, assuming it was off the record, am I likely to hear it on your show the next day?' And it sort of stopped him for a moment. And he sort of thought for a second and then he said, almost ashamedly, 'Yeah, I guess you probably could. When I go into my on-air personality. . . .' he said, not finishing the sentence. It's almost as if he can't fully control it, which is a little insight into himself. You get the feeling that he may well say it, and even feel a little bit sorry that he had, but that it's a price he's willing to pay to be true to his image or comic mask or whatever you call it, just to get pretentious."

Does it bother Cavett when Howard talks about him on the air? "No, it amuses me. And usually after his worst insults he'll absolve things by adding, 'But he's a good guy.' Usually I just have a tone with Howard, like congratulating him on his ability to sustain a constant low level of humor. He's the hard hat's Voltaire.

"I think his glasses are important because he has rather sweet, feminine eyes, which sort of belie his supposed aggressiveness. They look sort of sweet, sort of weak vision eyes. And there's something slightly feminine about them and soft. He'll love that I said that but it's true. He looks like a very different person without his glasses. Wearing his glasses changes his personality more to the one he's selling.

"It's an enormous amount of work he goes through each day. I can't imagine how anybody can sustain the man-hours at that level without getting bored. Robin is a big help. She is very skillful at keeping the ball in the air. I still don't think

Howard is a flash in the pan. I give him another six months more."

David Lee Roth, the former lead singer of Van Halen has popped up on Howard's show from time to time. Recently, Mr. Roth was arrested in Washington Square Park down in the Village for buying a $10 bag of pot. I remember thinking to myself, "Why would he be dumb enough to buy his own pot in such a public place?" Apparently, Howard wondered the same thing and called the rock star on the phone. According to the *New York Post*'s Page Six, Roth told Howard that he just did it out of habit. For all intents and purposes, possession of marijuana had been decriminalized. "It's like buying a pretzel and a soda pop on a Sunday afternoon," Roth explained. His fine would be only $35. "Hey, if your dog poops on the street and you don't clean it up, it's $100."

Another talented musician, Nils Lofgren, best known for playing with Bruce Springsteen for several years, also appeared on Howard's program several times. Nils is short in height, and Howard and the gang go out of their way to make fun of this fact, merely in an effort to get Lofgren's goat. Howard, who is tall to begin with, towers over the diminutive musician. So somehow, and I'm not sure who issued the challenge, a bet was made over who would win in a one-on-one basketball game. Howard would be the first to admit that he is no athlete, and no one would ever deny that fact. But based solely on his height advantage, he figured he could whip this cocky little rocker. So they agreed to play hoops on Howard's Channel 9 TV show.

Naturally, Howard spiced and hyped it up. He had on sexy cheerleaders for him and not-so-sexy cheerleaders for Nils, and some curious fans in the bleachers, including Lloyd Lindsay Young and George Lindsay Young, two local father and son weathermen. Whether it was to build up the anticipation or simply prolong the inevitable, Howard delayed the game for about a half hour.

Finally, the sporting event began, and to put it mildly, it was embarrassing. Howard was pathetic on the court. Nils, who obviously is a talented basketball player, looked like the best player in the universe next to Howard. Howard scored a few, but in the end he got his butt whipped. He took the loss in less than humble fashion, but definitely good-naturedly. Nils, if I recall correctly, was a bit arrogant in victory. But then Howard let him sing his newest song, which was great, and everyone was happy afterwards.

Curtis and Lisa Sliwa founded the Guardian

Angels, a group of young men and women who patrol the streets of New York City in an effort to protect its citizens from criminals. They now have offshoot groups all around the country.

Lisa, at the beginning, was the only female member. She was also a fashion model. She and Curtis used to come on Howard's show quite often, and it was always fun because Lisa used to boss tough Curtis around. One time she even kicked him down a set of stairs, which sent Howard into hysterics. The Sliwas apparently had an unusual marriage. I believe they had separate apartments, and Lisa used to claim that she wouldn't let Curtis sleep with her.

But the Sliwas are no longer regular guests. According to the *Washington Post,* Curtis got angry with Howard. He said he was tired of the constant phone calls. "He kept calling Lisa, wanting her to go on the air with him. Finally I had to introduce him to Mr. Click," Curtis said, gesturing with his hand as if he were slamming down a phone.

Six

Friend and Foes

Definitely falling into the previously mentioned category of unusual friendships is the team of Gene Siskel and Roger Ebert, those famous thumbs-up movie critics. And I don't mean the fact that they are friends, which by the way they are. I'm talking about their unlikely friendship, or at least mutually admiring relationship, with Howard. Howard seems to really enjoy talking to these guys, and they happen to be consistently entertaining guests, both on the radio and even on his Channel 9 show (where Howard had a pretty spokesmodel sit on a slightly embarrassed Roger's lap).

The three of them come pretty equally armed for what always turns out to be a fun battle of wits. It's also enjoyable to see these film critics having such a good time so far outside of what we perceive to be their natural element.

I talked to each of them separately. Roger recalls their first venture to the Howard Stern radio show.

"Gene and I wanted to be on the show. We had not yet heard Howard at that time but we knew him by reputation. And we were out promoting our show. Howard's show is sort of like other shows of the same nature. Basically there is a pretty steady format across the country, where you had the Big Banana and the Second Banana, or the Big Cheese and the Second Banana. Of course, many shows around the country have incorporated reality radio where the broadcast is about the broadcast. Howard is a complete original, but his format is not original. He does keep me listening, though."

What's it like going on with Howard? "If you can't stand the heat, get out of the kitchen. You have no business being on that show if you can't take the heat, unless you are ready to deal with Howard. It's a stimulating experience. It is not boring."

So, was Roger as embarrassed as he seemed when that girl sat on his lap during Howard's TV show? "Howard had a spokesmodel come and sit on my lap. I was uncomfortable only because I didn't think of what I should have done, which was to tell her, 'Thanks very much, but now it's your turn to sit on Gene Siskel's lap.'" When I told Gene about Roger's comment, he shot back, "It's funny. Roger is always thinking of what he should have done, after the fact. It's very difficult for him."

Anyway, back to Roger: "If you look at that particular TV show you'll see that we held our own pretty effectively. That's part of the fun of doing his show. Howard makes for a worthy adversary."

True to his nature, Roger starts critiquing Howard. "If you look around the Museum of Television and Radio, you will find some of Howard's sources and predecessors. The people who really created this entire genre of radio are Bob and Ray. They used to do Wally Balloo, the feckless interviewer. Before them, radio, generally speaking, played it pretty straight. And before that, the most far-out guy was probably Fred Allen. Then in the early 1950s there was this coming together all at once where you had Bob and Ray, Stan Freberg, and *Mad* magazine. All three of which popularized the very satirical and self-referential view of the media. Howard Stern is carrying on in that tradition. The tradition obviously existed before Howard, but Howard is an individual and what he does is who he is.

"I believe that the Howard Stern you hear on the radio is a fictitious character, very much so, in his imagination. I believe that when he goes home to his wife and family he is a great deal more conventional than his public persona. For example, I'm sure that as a parent giving advice to his children, Howard would give the same advice that his mother or father would have given him."

"It's always spontaneous when we go on Howard's show. We don't plan anything in advance. We just do whatever happens. We have fun. Once I shouted something at Howard, and he turned off my microphone. So I walked around his desk and used his microphone. A guest had never thought of doing that before, because Howard would never turn off his own mike. I really enjoy going on the show, and I plan to do it again the next time I'll be in New York." Hopefully, that will be soon.

Ladies and gentlemen, Mr. Gene Siskel: "I think Howard can be really funny, and what I like about him more than his shock jock value is sometimes he can cut through a lot of phoniness and deal with things very directly. I appreciate that."

Gene seems like a cool, confident guy, so it's not too surprising to find that he doesn't go into Howard's show with trepidation. "I go in with an expectation of having a good time and I always do. I'm not afraid of him and I feel I can hold my own with him and I always do."

I think Gene and Roger hold their own against Howard better than anyone else. "I would think so." Does it make it more of a challenge each time he goes there? "I'm sure it makes it more of a challenge for *him*.

"We both like him and he knows that, and he likes us and we know that, so it's all fun. The only time I get frustrated is when I spot him being phony or argumentative just for the sake of it. He'll hold an opinion just to be contrary or to pick a fight. He's smarter than he lets on. We let him know when we see through his act. But I don't really know him off the air, and I don't even listen to his program that often. I don't listen to a lot of radio, period.

"One time I did forty-five minutes on the phone with Howard, and Roger wasn't around. I still held my own with him. And it was much more enjoyable because Roger wasn't there.

"We've done the [Channel 9] TV show, which was kind of funny and very strange, but basically we have a pure radio relationship and it works, and we sort of mutually enjoy each other, all three of us."

What does he think about Howard's movie, *The Adventures of Fartman?* "Like all films, if it's a hit he's a hero; if it bombs he's a jerk. Am I looking forward to seeing it? Yes, to some degree, I think. Sure I am, because I think he has a chance to do something different, instead of the same tired old thing like everybody else. My only question is will he be juvenile or smart, smarter than he lets on? I think he can be both outrageous and smart."

How would Siskel critique his appearances on Howard's show? "I think I can be objective about it, and say that we do make for entertaining radio. Frankly, I find doing the radio show (rather than the TV) is more enjoyable. There's more freedom on radio."

And is Gene a Howard Stern fan? "That is correct. I think he is fresh, and I think that he has to guard against getting stale." I don't think we have to worry too much on that front.

Not sometimes, but most of the time, we wonder not only how does Howard get this caliber of people on his show, but why do these people come on his show. Sure, most of the time it's the whoring principle, where someone comes on merely to promote a current project. But that's not always the case. For some guests, I imagine they come on merely because it's a lot of fun. That's not to say that their lives are otherwise boring, just that in spite of the embarrassing and humiliating potential, going on Howard's show is worth the trouble.

Which brings us to former Mayor of New York City, Ed Koch. It is and it isn't surprising that Mr. Koch and Mr. Stern get along. Koch was an aggressive, no-bullshit mayor, who seldom pulled any punches. He was also quite popular, until he finally lost his job to Mayor David Dinkins. In response to this obvious public blunder, Mr. Koch, who is no fan of Dinkins, says, "I'll never come back to office. The people threw me out, and they must be punished."

But what about Howard Stern? "I am a fan of Howard Stern. I think he is a genius. When I was mayor, they called me many times to be on his show and I would say, 'No, I like Howard Stern and I think he does a terrific job, but I don't want to go on his show because he talks dirty and I'm the mayor and people just don't want me to do that, so I'm not going to do it. And I have nothing against Howard and he just has to understand that.'

"So, I thereby avoided going on several times. And then one day he called up and said that it was his birthday, and his mother and father were going to be at his party and it was going to be in the Village at some restaurant/cabaret and would I come for breakfast. And I said, 'Howard, you talk dirty. I can't go on your program.' So he said he promised not to talk dirty while I was there. So I said, 'Then I'll come. It's your birthday, sure.' So I went and he kept his promise. I met his mother and father, and he didn't talk dirty.

"We just sort of hit it off. He's always been nice to me in his comments and I've always said very nice things about him, because he's sort of a seminal force like Lenny Bruce was, and that's why it's criminal for the FCC to be doing what they are doing.

"I was recently on his program. Now I don't care whether he talks dirty or not. I'm not the mayor anymore. But I very rarely listen to the show, because I go to the gym, then my law office, then I have my own radio show, and I have a column at the [New York] *Post*."

So, does this incredibly busy man have fun on Howard's show? "Oh yes, it is a fun experience in the studio. He and Robin have a very easy camaraderie. He just knows how to handle a guest and audience very well."

During a recent broadcast, while actor Corey Feldman was on the air, Willie Nelson called in. Willie was actually going to be doing Howard's E! "interview" show later that day, but apparently he just couldn't wait to talk to Howard. Howard immediately zeroed in on Willie's financial situation and his lovemaking prowess. What else?! Apparently, Howard read an article where one of Willie's former lovers claimed that after making love Willie did a backflip. "That guitar is a tookie magnet. Just look at Joe Walsh," Howard said in analyzing this phenomenon. Also, Willie allegedly can make love for up to nine hours. Howard, after commenting on how tough it is to live up to that article, wanted to know if that nine hours included Willie preening his beard. "You know what," Howard said, "if I could last nine hours I wouldn't pay much attention to my finances either."

Willie has been married numerous times, which also baffles Howard. "Why marry them?!" Then Howard tries to bait Willie into commenting on some of his contemporaries, but it is Howard that does most of the commenting: "That Billy Ray Cyrus! It's like having your gym teacher getting a hit song." "Wouldn't you like to pound Garth Brooks on his hat? See how far down that hat sinks?" "Tell Kris (Kristofferson) not to shave off that beard. He looks sick when he does. Like he ate bad food." "Me and Willie both look like we're homeless, except Willie almost was."

For those of you who don't know who Morton Downey, Jr., is — well, consider yourselves lucky. Although to tell the truth, during his fifteen minutes of intense fame, he was hard to ignore. But he was always hard to take for any length of time. He had his own talk show of sorts, where he would have on controversial guests and then Morton would incite the already primed crowd, and we'd have an hour of shouting, shoving, and threatening. It was at the very least a curious phenomenon while it lasted.

Downey made for some memorable moments on Howard's program, whether as a guest or during a fracas with Stuttering John where Morton punched John.

Anyway, during one particular bit, Howard had Morton on as a guest, and he put on Morton's former secretary which resulted in an X-rated exchange.

Now Pat Cooper, a hilarious middle-aged comedian, is a true character. There is no way he has time to think before he speaks, because the words come pouring out of his mouth at supersonic speed. He can pop a blood vessel over any topic, and therefore qualifies to be a frequent visitor to the Howard Stern Show. Pat is another one of those guys you wouldn't think would come on Howard's program, but these two have developed an undeniable bond.

Howard loves that Pat speaks his mind. He never edits, no matter what the repercussions may be. Sometimes, as happens with many of Howard's guests, Pat gets a little bit out of control. But out of control is what the Howard Stern show is all about, so no one gets too upset. As long as it boosts the ratings, as Howard would say.

Of course, the most memorable moments with Pat involved the on-air battles he had with several members of his estranged family, including his son and daughter, and even his mother.

One day Howard arranged for Pat's son Mike to call in, in hopes of patching up this father and son relationship, or in hopes of creating some major fireworks. Whichever came first would be okay by Howard and company. Mike felt he was emotionally and financially abandoned by his father, but Pat doesn't fall for any emotional blackmail. Sometimes the exchange got pretty intense.

It continued on like that, but whether it was during this particular conversation or a future one, Pat and his son did get together, at least for awhile.

Do you know who Marilyn Michaels is? During the seventies and maybe even some of the eighties, she was real big. She was one of the few, if not the only, female impressionists around. She did an incredible Barbra Streisand and a convincing Joan Rivers. She was good and was a regular on both "The Ed Sullivan Show" and "The Tonight Show." Recently, her career got a lift when she appeared on Broadway in the appropriately titled *Catskills on Broadway.*

Now that you know who she is, we can go on with a fun bit she once did when Howard was out in Los Angeles for the Grammys. You already know she does Joan Rivers. So Howard decided to have Marilyn, posing as Joan, give K-Rock general manager Tom Chiusano a call to complain about Howard, and see if they could fake him out.

She went on and on, and Tom was apologetic and bought into it big time. When Michaels hung up, Howard and company were in hysterics. She then tried calling him again, this time pretending to be Dr. Ruth Westheimer, but I think Tom finally caught on.

Seems like a natural point to talk about Joan Rivers. Joan has certainly had a roller coaster career. She was perhaps the hottest comedienne for many years. For awhile, she was the permanent guest host for "The Tonight Show," when Johnny would take his endless vacation days. She was big; she was popular; she was, and still is, funny.

But then came the Fox deal, where she got her own talk show, going head-to-head (at least for a half hour) with Carson. Apparently, Joan didn't discuss this with Johnny first, and when he found out about it, at the same time all of America did, he was livid. The country was split on the way Joan handled things.

Though the actual reasons why are a bit sketchy, Joan's show went off the air. Her husband Edgar later killed himself, which Joan blamed on the pressure Fox put on him (he produced her show). Then, as the saying goes, Joan Rivers couldn't get arrested. Her career had virtually hit rock bottom.

But over the last several years, she has pulled herself up and is doing quite well these days. She has her own daytime talk show, a gossip show, a line of jewelry, and a newfound popularity. Joan is definitely back.

Now, after Joan left Fox, Arsenio Hall took over her hosting duties on the late night show. And one fateful day, Howard Stern was going to be a guest on that show. Once on air though, Howard launched into an attack on the Fox executives and how they were responsible for Edgar Rosenberg's death. Well, according to Howard's on-air recollections about the event, during the commercial break Howard was escorted off the show.

So here lies the affinity between these two performers. But it's still curious that Joan Rivers would ever find her way onto the Howard Stern Show, especially considering the blunt way Howard talks about her dead husband and other personal areas.

But it's one of those many cases where Howard will bad-mouth someone until they call or show up on his program. Once he feels accepted by the people he maligns, he can start liking them. It's a strange thing, and I believe a little insight into the mind of Howard Stern.

So, since Joan first surprised Howard by calling in, the two have become great friends. She does his show; he does her show; he still makes fun of her and her jewelry line, and probes into her sex life. But underneath it all seems to lie a genuine caring about one another.

Speaking of talk show hosts, Howard could find himself in a bit of a dilemma: Dave or Jay? Jay or Dave? Yes, when David Letterman moves to CBS to go head-to-head with Jay Leno, Howard is going to have to choose between them. Unless, of course, there is no booking war between the two hosts, which considering the stakes involved seems highly unlikely.

David Letterman gave Howard his first national exposure, and Howard has been on Letterman's late night show quite a few times. But Dave and Howard have a love/hate thing going on that always makes their relationship a bit unclear.

When I hear that Howard is going to be on Letterman I get that sense of nervous excitement I used to experience when I'd witness Lucy Ricardo do something that was about to get her in trouble.

In other words, danger is always close at hand when Stern and Letterman meet. Of course, it makes for great television, which is probably why Dave has let Howard come on so many times. It's hard to know just how Dave really feels about anyone, but in Howard's case it's even more enigmatic. There are moments where Dave seems to be genuinely pleased to have Howard on his show, but then there are the more frequent occasions where Dave looks as if he wishes he were anywhere else but sitting next to this crazy radio personality. The time Howard stuck his bare foot in Dave's face is probably one of those moments.

According to *USA Today*, back in January of this year, Howard was discussing the Leno/Letterman issue and whose show he'll go on. "On the one hand, I owe allegiance to Letterman because Letterman put me on first and treated me like a human being. But the last time I was on Letterman, he looked at me after I was done and said, 'What's wrong with you? You just used the word fart on my television show.' And I said, 'What is it? You're being courted by CBS and you've now become a member of the religious right?' So I don't know where I stand with Letterman."

Jay Leno, on the other hand, used to call in or

drop by on Howard's show long before he became the regular host of "The Tonight Show with Jay Leno." Jay always came across as a nice guy.

Once Jay got the word that he was taking over the show, Howard saw his golden opportunity. Sure he's done Letterman, but "The Tonight Show's" audience is far larger, and therefore more people for Howard to outrage, whine to, embarrass, or even make laugh.

He started campaigning heavily to be on, and Jay told him that he would absolutely have Howard on as a guest. This initiated some major ass kissing on Howard's part. That is, at least, until a few small problems arose. Howard had certain demands. He wanted to be on first, and Helen Kushnick, Jay's manager and the show's then producer, couldn't make any guarantees. Well, no one puts off Howard Stern without hearing about it on his show.

Anyway, to cut to the chase, Howard finally had a date set to be on Jay's show. In the horrible event that you might have missed Howard's appearance, let me tell you it was a night to remember. Certainly, Jay Leno will never forget it.

During the monologue, Jay described Howard as the "always annoying Howard Stern." Then, during his intro to Howard, Jay said, "Now to prove that we here are *not* members of the cultural elite, Howard Stern!" Howard came out to the screams of the crowd, then true to form, took control.

Howard told Jay right away that "this is truly marking a beginning, having me on. I think it shows a difference in direction for 'The Tonight Show.' I think it's a loosening up of 'The Tonight Show,' if I may say." He then told the audience that Jay talked to him backstage and asked him not to mention Johnny Carson. Jay didn't feel comfortable having Howard roast Johnny on his show.

Howard agreed.

But then, instead, he caught Jay off guard when he homed in on Ed McMahon and Doc Severinsen as his two targets. He called them the two biggest loads in show business, then went into a wild tirade about them kissing up to Arsenio Hall on "The Arsenio Hall Show." Howard was outraged on Jay's behalf. But try as he might he couldn't get Jay to say a disparaging word about Arsenio (that was to follow later in a war of words), Doc, or Ed.

"That's your whole problem, Jay. You're too nice a guy. You don't have the killer instinct," Howard told the befuddled host, who at one point tried to hide behind his desk. Howard even tried to bring Branford Marsalis, Jay's band leader, into the action by asking him what he thought about Arsenio. When Branford demurred, Howard said, "Oh, what is this, Branford? That he's a black guy and you're a black guy? So what? He's out to ruin you!" Branford, in turn, responded, "Hey man, I'm leaving it between the two white guys, all right?" Howard can't believe he is the only one who hates Arsenio. He then continues about "traitors" Ed McMahon ("that big fat blubber") and Doc Severinsen ("Crummy musician") going on Arsenio's show. "Let them go kiss Arsenio's ass. We don't need them. Screw 'em! Screw 'em!" Needless to say, the crowd went wild over Howard's tirade.

Jay temporarily regained enough control of his show to ask Howard some questions. He wondered if Howard's wife Alison ever got embarrassed by some of Howard's on-air talk about their private lives. Howard responded, "Jay, I think you can answer that best. What woman wouldn't want to be Mrs. Howard Stern?" The crowd screamed its approval once again.

But even after Howard's segment was over, he never relinquished control back to Jay. Singer Lyle Lovett followed with a great tune called, "She Makes Me Feel Good," then sat down and tried to talk with Stern's looming presence only inches away.

Next came on a young actress by the name of Anne-Marie Johnson. She wisely and immediately tried to ingratiate herself with Howard, not Jay. While she was talking to Jay, however, Howard started to fondle an embarrassed but

Howard's Southside High School
yearbook picture.

Southside High School in Rockville Centre, Long Island, New
York, where Howard finished his low profile high school years.

Howard and his wife, Allison in 1986. (*Albert Ferreira/D.M.I.*)

Robin Quivers, Howard's sexy sidekick.

"Stuttering" John Melendez, man-on-the-street celebrity interviewer for the show.

The entire crew: Robin, Howard, Fred, Jackie, Boy Gary Dell'Abate, and "Stuttering" John. (*Albert Ferreira/D.M.I.*)

Jackie "The Joke Man" Martling, who writes rapid-fire one-liners for Howard during the day and hones his skills doing stand-up comedy at night.

Fred Norris, a "wild man" of many talents, instruments, and voices.

Howard at the 1987 New York rally protesting the FCC's censorship with Grampa Al. (*Wide World Photos, Inc.*)

Howard answering the press about the demise of his late night TV show on local New York station WWOR-TV. (*Wide World Photos, Inc.*)

Howard, with fan "Melrose" (holding sign) at 1992 mock funeral for rival jocks Mark and Brian in Los Angeles. (*Nanook Millet/Globe Photos, Inc.*)

Howard and Tom Snyder. (*Globe Photos, Inc.*)

Howard and Joan Rivers. (*Albert Ferreira/D.M.I.*)

Howard and David Letterman. *(Globe Photos, Inc.)*

Howard with the comedian
Henny Youngman.
(Alex Oliveira/D.M.I.)

Howard and Jay Leno. *(Wide World Photos, Inc.)*

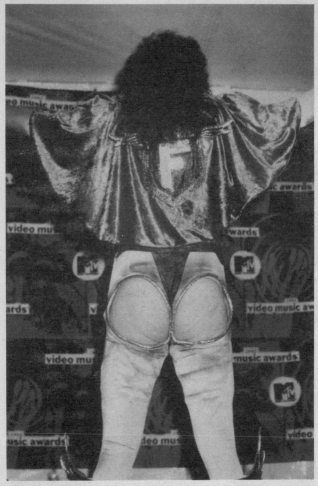

Howard as "Fartman" for all the world to see.

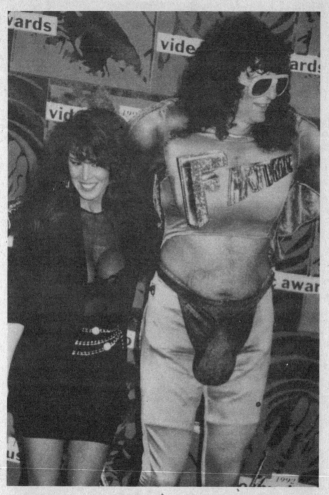

"Fartman" as Howard with Jessica Hahn at the 1992 MTV awards.

Howard made his motion picture debut as Ben Wah, the wacky television commentator in the 1986 dectective spoof RYDER P.I. (*Courtesy of Karl Hosch*)

Howard's celebrity guests:

Richard Lewis, comic and co-star of "Anything But Love." (*Ralph Dominguez/Globe Photos, Inc.*)

Gene Siskel and Roger Ebert, film critics. (*John Barrett/Globe Photos, Inc.*)

Howard's celebrity guests, continued:

"The Donald" Trump. (*John Barrett/Globe Photos, Inc.*)

Jon Bon Jovi. (*Adam Scull/Globe Photos, Inc.*)

Dick Cavett.
(*Adam Scull/Globe Photos, Inc.*)

Richard Simmons.
(*Michael Ferguson/ Globe Photos, Inc.*)

Howard's celebrity guests, continued:

Sam Kinison. (*Baret Lepejian/Globe Photos, Inc.*)

Gilbert Gottefried. (*Stephen Trupp/Globe Photos, Inc.*)

Geraldo Rivera.
(*John Barrett/Globe Photos, Inc.*)

Donna Albanese aka
Rachel the Spanker.

Howard Stern, shock jock extraordinaíre.

amused Lyle, which as you can imagine disrupted the by now inane conversation Jay was trying to have with Anne-Marie. Howard said that if this was his show he'd already be spanking Anne-Marie. Jay lost control, and it was wonderful. Jay then came out with a good one when he said to his brave female guest, "You know, I feel like we're having drinks at a bar, and there's a drunk at the end of the bar. There's like a moron at the end of the bar, and Lyle is the salesman from out of town who just came down to have a nightcap."

It was without a doubt great TV. And it certainly was one of the best "The Tonight Show with Jay Leno" broadcasts we're ever likely to see. Jay may have felt uncomfortable, but he's smart enough to realize that having Howard on was a great ratings move.

Seven

Tit for Tat

The crazy, wildly irreverent, overtly sexual Sandra Bernhard, who used to make frequent appearances on both Howard's and Letterman's shows, has been disappointingly scarce these days. I always enjoyed her appearances on Howard's show, especially because she can far outshock Howard.

But then back in November 1992 a *New York Newsday* article reported that Sandra had severed all ties with Howard. Apparently, the trouble began when Howard would constantly mock and ridicule Roseanne and Tom Arnold, who just so happened to be Sandra's colleagues on "Roseanne."

According to Ms. Bernhard, Howard had agreed to promote her upcoming show at the Paramount Theater as long as Sandra would call in on occasion. She told *Newsday* that she held up her end of the bargain, but Howard did not. "I've done him a lot of favors and this time the focus was not on what I needed it to be. And besides I don't need him to start trashing the people who employ me. Some of those phone-ins are big jerkoffs for me. They're adolescent trips. He should be happy that Tom and Roseanne gave me a regular gig to show my talent."

Speaking of Roseanne, though she's never been on Howard's show, the two do communicate through the media. Back on April 10, 1992, Howard was making one of his Letterman appearances when he started discussing Roseanne and Tom. According to the *New York Post,* Howard called Roseanne a "big, fat slob" and called Tom "the Yoko of the 1990s." The fact that Dave didn't jump in to defend Roseanne caused a rift between him and the queen of sitcoms. Roseanne, for her part, calls Howard a "barking frog" and a "hairy, angry troll." "I don't need to be seen by Dave's prisoners or Howard Stern's audience who are plumbers (masturbating) in their trucks on their way to work. I have better ratings in a half hour than either of them have in months. They can kiss my ass." She's also sick of Howard's people "coming to my hotel in New York and leaving seventy-five pizzas outside my door just because we're fat."

This one's a classic moment. Back in 1989 when Howard was broadcasting from Hollywood's Roosevelt Hotel while covering the Grammys, Howard spotted comedienne Elayne Boosler. He immediately started yelling at her through a bullhorn because she always refused to come on his radio program. Apparently, she wasn't thrilled with Howard because he made fun of her "Don't let them see you sweat" deodorant commercials she was doing. Anyway, while Howard continued his verbal barrage, Elayne's boyfriend/manager Steve Gerbson went over and asked him to stop. After some words went back and forth, Gerbson shoved the bullhorn in Howard's face. I remember Boy Gary jumping in to save his boss. I think Gary might have also taken a punch during the on-air fracas. It was all over in a moment, but it gave Howard and company enough material to get through the rest of the show.

Way back in November 1989, according to a *New York Post* article, Kirk Douglas's actor-turned-comedian son Eric Douglas came on Howard's show and participated in a Dial-A-Date. Perhaps in jest, but maybe not, Douglas said he was looking for a woman who would be willing to have sex with him on the very first date.

Elisa Shumofsky called into the show and after some flirtatious banter, won the date.

In May, 1992, Douglas came back on Howard's show and bragged that he was still seeing Ms. Shumofsky and that she was "great in bed."

Well, Shumofsky took exception to Douglas's remarks and ended up filing an $11-million defamation suit which named Douglas, Howard, Robin, Boy Gary, and, of course, the parent company Infinity Broadcasting. Her claim is that she has been "shunned and . . . suspected" by friends and family since Douglas made his post-date comments.

The legal game of shuffle board didn't end there. Shumofsky's lawsuit prompted Infinity to file countersuits against Shumofsky and Douglas.

"It is outrageous that Howard Stern can put a microphone in front of a guest, then sue that guest because of the conversation that Stern stimulated," raged Douglas's spokesman, Steve Mangione. "It amazes me that Mr. Stern thinks he can get away with picking on a young, hard-working, struggling performer," he continued according to the *Post* article.

During his third appearance on the show in June, 1992, Douglas told Howard that he got in a lot of trouble the last time he was on, Howard responded by saying, "Who even knows if he's been in bed with her? That's the point. He might say that. It doesn't mean he's been in bed with her."

Besides the bucks, poor Ms. Shumofsky also wants an apology and a retraction from Eric Douglas.

It's no surprise then that Douglas filed his own countersuit against Infinity and Shumofsky. Why should he be left out? His suit claims that Howard didn't tell him about the Dial-A-Date segment until he was already on the air, and that it was Shumofsky's conduct which prompted his remarks in the first place.

One of Howard's major coups, at least as far as he's concerned, was when Demi Moore called into his show from her car phone.

Howard, like most guys, has the hots for Demi and talks about her alot on his show. But he also bad-mouths Bruce Willis in the process. So when Demi called in, she proved to be a good sport, merely laughing and refusing to answer when Howard asked his typically ultra-personal questions. At one point, Howard said something that he thought must have been too offensive because suddenly Demi hung up on him. But it turned out the connection was broken while she went through a tunnel. Howard said it was a good thing he didn't say anything bad about her during that interim because she was still listening to the show.

Howard made fun of Emilio Estevez, Demi's one-time fiance. She defended her husband Bruce Willis, and I believe Howard quickly tempered what he had been saying about Bruce.

Another good sport, and frequent and surprising caller, is Alec Baldwin. He's a straight talker and a colorful guest. But whenever Howard talks to Alec, or even to Alec's brother Stephen, the subject always turns to Kim Basinger. Howard wants to know all there is to know about this "sexciting" actress. Alec usually laughs raucously or pretends to get mad when Howard asks an explicit question, but he usually has fun even while suffering the abuse. The last time I heard Alec on the program, he promised to try to get Kim to come down to Howard's show. (Howard was in Los Angeles at the time.) Just the prospect of that event happening got Howard in a tizzy, but to no one's surprise Kim never materialized.

Not only has Luke Perry, that 90210 heartthrob, been on Howard's show, but he has also been permanently linked to Howard's Fartman character. In a brilliantly disgusting display, Howard's Fartman made a gaseous appearance at last year's MTV Awards. "Flying" in, Howard, looking beefier than usual, yelled out to the crowd, "Yes, it is I. Fartman!" The crowd seemed to love it. It certainly was a showstopper. Who else would let millions of viewers see his cellulite-ridden butt cheeks hanging out in all their splendor, or his spare-tire belly hanging over his Fartman pants? It wasn't pretty, but it was pure Fartman. It was Luke who announced the entrance of Fartman and once Fartman made his landing, he bid Luke to touch his butt cheeks for power. We all watched in amazement as Luke gathered up his inner strength and then with both hands reached over and grabbed Fartman's ass.

At that moment I became a Luke Perry fan.

Howard respects George Carlin. Of course, George came up with the famous "seven dirty words" you're not supposed to say, which in his act he said repeatedly. Carlin is one of the best observational comics ever, and has lived on the edge for almost as far back as his career goes.

Howard wants to be accepted and even revered by comics, a group he is on the fringe of. So when George called in while Pat Cooper was in the studio with Howard, Howard asked him boldly, "Who's funnier, me or Lenny Bruce?" To Howard's chagrin, George said Lenny Bruce was funnier, but Howard did get him to admit that Howard at least has a dangerous edge. George admits to listening to Howard's show. "I even carry the radio around with me when I'm listening to your show because I don't want to miss a KA-BOOM!!" Both George and Pat agree that Howard is funnier than Chevy Chase, but George can't choose between Howard and Letterman. "I can't compare. I don't know." Howard makes it easy for him by telling George, "I am funnier than Letterman." What about Jay Leno? As a broadcaster, they both agree Howard is better. Then Howard asks the topper, "Who would you follow into a burning building, me or (the dead cult leader) David Koresh?" But the ever-political George goes one better when he comments, "Any time government guys and cult leaders are killing each other I'm a happy guy."

Plain and simple, Tom Snyder would never be a guest on the Howard Stern Show. It is one of life's little ironies then that Howard ended up being on a show with Tom. Howard was scheduled to be on "Later," the entertaining half hour interview show hosted by Bob Costas. But, for whatever reason, Bob was off that particular night and filling in for him was the loud, colorful, and once controversial Tom Snyder.

A true professional, Tom could have easily gotten through the entire interview without even a hint of his real feelings for Howard shining through. But, in case you forgot, Howard "Mr.

Honesty" Stern was there to bring out the truth at all costs. And we got a show to remember in the process.

Almost immediately, Howard wants to lay the cards on the table. Tom begins to ask Howard some probing question, and Howard interrupts and says, "Are we going to work out this thing between us first before you go into this serious interview?" To which Tom replied, "There's nothing between us, pal. We do this half hour and we never see each other again."

It went on like that for the entire half hour. I have never seen the likes of it before or since. It was a great battle between two very strong-minded, stubborn men, each at the opposite end of the spectrum. Here's an edited version of some of their barbed exchanges:

Howard (H): You have bad rapped me before. I have read articles that you said you don't like what I do. Is that true?

Tom (T): I have said that I am not a fan of your format. I do not care for what is called shock radio. The kind of things you and others do on radio, I am not a fan of.

H: You don't think I'm funny?

T: No, I don't. I don't think you're funny. I watched a cassette of your television show last night and you had on Lesbian Dating Game, you talked about the Sammy Davis

Cancer Man. You know this is all funny stuff to some people. Pal, to me it's not funny. Now that does not make you unfunny. It makes me . . .

H: It makes you out of touch.

T: I admit that.

H: I think you do like me. I think you're afraid to admit that you like me. Because there is something inside us all. Something evil inside us all that likes me. The idea of my show is to convey real honesty on the air. To get away from the phony type of broadcasting where someone sits there and bites their tongue and are afraid to say anything. If I were interviewing you I'd love to know about your days at NBC. I'd love to know your problems at NBC.

T: But you also want to know my toilet habits.

H: Yeah, I would. What are your toilet habits?

T: I want to tell you, Howard, you got to get out more.

H: This is like two mental patients arguing! You know, guys like you want to broadcast in a phony style. You want everything nice, nothing provocative. You just want to go along, everything should be fine. No one should shock anybody with the truth. No one should do anything. All the network executives should be happy. To me, the exciting part of broadcasting is turning on that listener in his car. So he's trapped in his car for two hours, and you know he doesn't want to leave his car because he doesn't want to miss what we're doing.

(Talking about Howard's Channel 9 show, Howard says he got high ratings.)

T: Oh please, don't give me ratings, don't give me "beat 'Saturday Night live.' " Give me what you want the viewer to have. The viewer doesn't care about the ratings!

H: You are so combative! You must really want this job. My God, almighty. Why don't you relax? You're anal retentive.

T: I'm anal compulsive. Get it right.

H: Why don't you try to be nice? What the hell's the matter with you?

T: You are what is wrong with television.

Things descend even farther after this point, turning into a shouting match. Howard calls Tom a maniac and a psychopath, and says he should be in a mental hospital. At the end of the broadcast, after the sound went off, Tom throws a disgusted look and gesture at Howard and storms off the set. It sure looked genuine enough. Howard really got to him.

Jessica Hahn is, by now, a familiar name and face to Howard Stern listeners and viewers everywhere. Her involvement with Sam Kinison is legendary, her cosmetic surgery-enhanced body keeps getting sexier. She has posed several times for *Playboy* magazine, she has her own video out now which sexily tells the Jessica Hahn story. She had her own radio show for a while, and even hosted a bizarre TV show.

But lest we forget, today's Jessica evolved from the poor church secretary who scandalized the PTL with her revelation that she was sexually assaulted by Jim Bakker.

In 1980, the virginal Jessica was working for the PTL, and she loved it. She told *People* magazine, "Whatever I could do to make the ministers' job easier, I did. They represented God, and I loved God so much, and I respected them, and I wanted to make their job easier."

She had also worshipped Jim Bakker for years. So when John Fletcher, another PTL minister, invited Jessica to a PTL telethon in Florida, she was thrilled to go. It never occurred to her that it was all just a sexual trap. But that's what it was. Jessica said she was sexually abused in a Florida hotel by Bakker and Fletcher, and then accepted a

$265,000 settlement to keep quiet about the incident. She did this for seven long years.

But when the *Charlotte Observer* broke the story of what happened to her, she was relieved to get it out in the open. This disclosure, verified by Jessica, virtually ruined Jim and Tammy Faye Bakker's scam-built empire, and hurt the PTL organization right at its core.

It also took an enormous toll on Jessica. She was embarrassed and humiliated by public reaction to her statement. She was treated more like an accomplice and less like the victim she was.

According to *People* magazine, the next few months were a horror tale in which she found herself totally alone in the world and an object of mockery. She was afraid to venture out of her West Babylon, New York, apartment, for fear of the wall of reporters lurking outside. She felt betrayed by Jerry Falwell, the PTL's new leader. In her self-imposed imprisonment, she came frighteningly close to suicide.

She was befriended by "Nightline's" Ted Koppel. Then somehow, Howard got her phone number and called her up. Howard immediately became one of Jessica's most trusted confidantes, and Howard, for his part, tried to give Jessica some good advice. "With all his craziness," Jessica told *People,* "he was the only one to call and say, 'Jessica, are you okay?' He's a decent man."

The rest, as they say, is history. Jessica eventually befriended Hugh Hefner and posed for *Playboy.* Now she is a celebrity in her own right. And I think some of her willingness to take fun-minded abuse from Howard stems from her gratitude at his being there when she really needed some comfort in her life.

Howard is not the type to dwell on such things, but even he could sense the fragile, shaky times Jessica was going through when he first spoke to her on the phone. That was a long time ago, and Jessica has certainly come worlds away from that period in her life.

Recently featured in Howard's "Butt Bongo Fiesta," Jessica and her luscious body, remain loyal to Howard. She's a genuine character with a heart of gold. And to tell you the truth, sometimes I wish Howard would still treat her a little nicer and gentler. She's been through a lot.

And then there is Mary Jo Buttafuoco. Actually Joey Buttafuoco first called into Howard's show, but later Mary Jo did, and I think it gave the wrong impression to some people.

First of all, for the two people who aren't up-to-date on this, here's just a brief recap of this still current news story. On May 19, 1992, Mary Jo Buttafuoco answered the ringing doorbell of her

Massapequa, New York, home. According to a *People* magazine article, standing on the front porch was an attractive teenage girl named Amy Fisher. The girl said she wanted to talk to Mary Jo about her husband Joey. Amy said that Joey was having an affair with her sixteen-year-old sister. "I think the idea of a forty-year-old man sleeping with a sixteen-year-old is disgusting," Amy went on.

Mary Jo, keeping cool, smiled and said, "He's not forty yet." She then said she was going in to call Joey, but Amy Fisher didn't let her do that. Instead she pulled out a .25-caliber pistol and shot Mary Jo Buttafuoco in the head, leaving her for dead.

Mary Jo survived the attack, though she has nerve damage on the right side of her face, permanent hearing loss, and double vision.

As this bizarre case unfolded, the country became fascinated by this confusing scandal. Amy Fisher claimed that she and Joey were lovers. Joey, till this day, denies everything. Smart man. He admits to knowing Amy, but says he never had an affair with her. He says that she is a nut who fantasized that Joey loved her and that's why she shot Mary Jo, to get her out of the way.

Well, Howard obviously talked quite a bit about this case on his program. He got a lot of airplay out of it. Then, miraculously, one day Joey Buttafuoco called into the show to defend himself. He was joking around with Howard, and I am certain that this phone call didn't do much to help Joey's credibility with the prosecutor's office.

Anyway, Joey told Howard, "Look, Mary Jo's my high school sweetheart. I've been dying to be with a thirty-seven-year-old woman all my life. Now I finally got one. What the hell. Am I now going to go back with a sixteen- or seventeen-year-old throwback?"

It truly was an interesting line of defense. After the call, Howard said on air that he didn't believe Joey's tale but he advised him to stick with that crazy story. Months later, Mary Jo herself called in and told Howard that her sex life had never been better.

Howard, as you can imagine, used his "involvement" in the case for as long as possible. It is a curious phenomenon that people overwhelmed by tragic events would think to call into Howard. I'm not sure what they expect to accomplish by this. Either Howard's appeal is so strong that talking to him outweighs worrying about going to prison, or it just shows that the whole world is nuts and there's no point trying to explain anything. I think the second choice is much easier to handle.

Eight

Sam Kinison

The very first time I saw Sam Kinison perform was on an HBO comedians special hosted by Rodney Dangerfield. It had to be at least seven or eight years ago. Sam stood out right from the get-go. It wasn't just his loud, anguished scream that made him unique. It was his attitude, his obvious intelligence, and his hilarious anger.

After doing a bit about how once a guy gets married, he then has to hand over his dick to his wife if he wants to go out with the boys at night, and screaming about how he was cleaned out by former wives, Sam drew us in with a bit that started with convincing mock sincerity.

He said he'd like to take a moment to talk about world hunger, particularly the awful situation that was going on in Africa. He said, "I know how to cure the hunger situation over there. Really, I have the cure. Want to know what it is? (He then screams) MOVE WHERE THE FOOD IS! THIS IS SAND. NOTHING GROWS HERE!!!!"

I'll never forget how hard I laughed at that moment, nor forget the impact this short, heavy, bandanna-wearing, ex-preacher comic had on me then and up until the day he died. When he died, in what at the time seemed to be the most ironic of circumstances, I, like most of Sam's fans, felt like I had lost a friend. There was that quality about him. His wrath and his love were so loaded with conviction and sincerity that he became, in a way, an enigmatic symbol who made us cringe and think at the same time.

If ever there were two people who seemed fated to meet it was Sam and Howard. And the millions of Howard listeners will be forever grateful that their paths crossed, because Sam and Howard together made for some of the choicest radio moments in recent history.

Howard has had a multitude of comics and other celebrities on his show, but my personal favorite, and I know I'm not alone in this sentiment, was Sam Kinison. It still pains me, in a selfish sort of way, to know that I'll never get to hear Sam and Howard create any more radio magic.

That's why I love when Sam is featured on the "Best of Howard Stern," a compilation of Howard's classics that is run on the air when he's on vacation. I can also listen to him on the *Crucified by the FCC* tapes, the cassettes he made featuring uncensored bits. This guy was never a dud. Whether he went off on some amazingly articulate tirade on God-knows-what subject, or he came into the studio totally trashed from partying all night, as listeners, we could feel the electric potential in the air. We knew we were in for some kind of on-the-edge treat.

That's why Howard and Sam were such a perfect pair. Each greatly respected the other, while simultaneously knowing they could each push the other further than anyone else. They crossed the line many times over, but always were able to come back and find their friendship intact.

Of course, the Bon Jovi incident almost put an end to their strong, but mercurial, relationship. Howard gave rock icon Jon Bon Jovi and his band extensive air time when they were first starting out and barely known. Bon Jovi went on to become a mega-power group, and Howard loved that he knew them when they were nobodies. Now that they were somebodies he wanted what was fairly coming to him — respect and more recognition.

Anyway, the band did regularly stay in touch with Howard on the air for a while, but then their management company (so they claim) told them it was bad for their image to do the Howard Stern show, and basically, they just stopped coming by or talking with Howard on his radio program. Jon Bon Jovi tried to explain this reasoning to Howard, but he would have none of it.

And so began one of Howard's most famous feuds. And, as anyone who has been on Howard's hit list can tell you, it's not a pleasant place to be. Howard would bad-mouth his former friends, Bon Jovi, every chance he got, doing so with a foaming-at-the-mouth vehemence that seemingly would make any reconciliation impossible.

Enter Sam Kinison. Sam and Howard were already great friends, and Sam also happened to be friends with Jon Bon Jovi. So Sam decided to arrange a make up session between the two former friends, and both parties agreed. Howard even decided to hold a press conference to announce the patch up.

Howard set up the press conference, and neither Bon Jovi nor Sam Kinison show up. It was a big setup and Howard was the patsy. Howard was terribly angry and humiliated, and as devoted

Stern fans we shared his dishonor.

Needless to say both Bon Jovi and Sam became *persona non grata,* and victims of Howard's tongue-lashing.

On Sam's part, all indications are that he thought this was just a great joke, and that Howard, a great jokester himself, would get over the initial embarrassment and eventually appreciate the purity of the joke itself. But that didn't happen.

Sam and Howard got into a lengthy, heated, on-air argument about the "joke," and though nothing was resolved at the time, Howard was able to replay the conversation humorously as Fred counted how many times Howard and Sam said the words "man" and "dude."

Eventually tempers did die down, and though each injured party felt like he was the victim, both Sam and Howard missed each other. A reconciliation was in the making.

On the *Crucified by the FCC* tapes we are privy to a conversation that Sam and Jessica Hahn had on the air, the day Sam came in to make nice to Howard. You can tell that nerves were still a bit frayed at that point, and when Sam got a hold of the vulnerable Jessica he took out all of his anger on the poor woman.

I recall hearing this memorable program, but

obviously it was a somewhat edited version, since Howard had to hit the bleep button numerous times. Reference is made to Howard's and Sam's feud, but mostly it is vintage, unrehearsed Sam Kinison at his best, trading quick responses with Howard, Ronnie (Howard's limo driver), and Jessica Hahn.

As Howard said of Sam, "For my money, Sam Kinison is the greatest living comic mind. There's nobody better than Sam Kinison. What Sam does is he takes any situation and he makes it compelling. If you give Sam a good premise he'll just create radio magic. And Jessica will confront any situation honestly. And that's hard to do with millions of people listening to you on the radio."

Thankfully, Sam and Howard patched up their differences and resumed their strong friendship. When I heard the news that Sam had died, after my initial shock, I actually thought of Howard. I knew this would affect him deeply. Yet, at the same time, I wondered how Howard would deal with this on his program that coming Monday morning.

That night I tuned into Howard's TV program on Channel 9. I knew it was going to be a rerun so, of course, I didn't expect any mention of Sam. But right before the show aired, a worded message on the screen dedicated that night's show to Sam Kinison. It said something to the effect that "tonight's show is wild and irreverent. Just the way Sam would have liked it." It was a classy touch on Howard's part, and bespoke the sense of loss that Howard obviously felt.

That Monday, Howard dealt with this issue in the best way possible. Obviously, he acknowledged it right away and, as always, said what we pretty much were all feeling: "I just can't believe he's gone and that I'll never see him again."

It wasn't a somber program. It became, appropriately, a celebration of Sam and the great, fortunately numerous memories we have of him. Howard took calls from fans and reminisced about some of the memorable moments created by Sam and, most of the time, Howard. He planned an entire day devoted to classic Kinison, and that broadcast was immediately nostalgic, laced with both humor and sadness. It was a perfect tribute.

Howard also keeps Sam's name in our mouth and his image in our minds by talking with Sam's widow Maleeka, his brother Bill, and even Jessica. And, of course, there's always the "Best of Stern."

Besides living on through the "Best of Stern,"

Sam's legacy also continues through Howard's frequent recollections. Sam would be happy to know that Howard is more acerbic than reverential when discussing him. Recently, Howard tried to contact Sam through a medium, and asked if it would be alright for Howard to sleep with Maleeka. According to the medium, Sam said he would mind.

Howard would still be Howard without Sam Kinison, and there's no doubt he would still be as popular as he is now. But for my money, there has never been a better guest.

Nine

FCC Fiasco

Even non-listeners of Howard Stern must be aware by now of Howard's extensive problems with the FCC—Federal Communications Commission. And for us listeners, we have been subjected to hundreds of Howard's tirades against these "witch-hunters." Although some of his outbursts are a bit exaggerated in intensity, it sure sounds as if Howard is genuinely upset.

The FCC has fined Howard's parent company, Infinity Broadcasting, well over $600,000.

But Howard knows how to take a bad situation and make it work in his favor. First of all, Howard is fortunate enough to finally be working for a company that supports him and is willing to back that up. Infinity is fighting the charges and fines. It could take years before this gets out of litigation.

Meanwhile, Howard has turned this into a cause célèbre for himself. He is now the figurative poster boy for Free Speech, and many of his celebrity friends, and even some detractors, have sided with him.

His most vocal supporter, and one for which Howard is still pinching himself, is New York Senator Alfonse D'Amato. The senator even wrote to the FCC saying that these fines are "designed to muzzle Stern, and that is censorship plain and simple. While Howard Stern may not be everyone's cup of tea," D'Amato continues, "censorship is clearly not the American way."

According to *New York Newsday,* D'Amato actually feels the FCC should be eliminated. "What do we need an FCC for? What do they do? All they do is decide who's going to sell what." Instead, said D'Amato, "let the marketplace decide, and stop this business of trying to censor everything and everybody." The *New York Post* reports that D'Amato's letter marks the first time a high-ranking public official has responded to the FCC's efforts to clean up Stern's act.

Part of Howard's and his supporters' complaints involve the vagueness of the FCC guidelines. It used to be you simply couldn't mention the seven dirty words (made famous by George Carlin). Now, there doesn't seem to be any definitive rules, which is frustrating, to say the least, and perhaps unconstitutional, to say the most. In a *Rolling Stone* article, Howard made this comment regarding the FCC's vagueness, "All I'm saying is, don't give me a speeding ticket unless you can tell me what the speed limit is." Good quote.

Most of Howard's problems with the FCC began when the show started getting specific complaints from people who, in most cases, accidentally tuned into his program. In 1986 a woman named Mary Keeley heard Howard's on-air antics, was appalled at his lewdness, and then contacted the infamous Donald Wildmon, then President of the National Federation for Decency (now it's called the American Family Association). Together they filed the first serious complaint with the FCC against Howard Stern.

Then, as chronicled in a *New York* magazine piece, in 1988 a New Jersey woman named Anne Stommel woke up to 92.3 K-Rock instead of WPAT. What a difference a fraction on your radio dial can make! Inadvertently, Ms. Stommel was introduced to Howard Stern's unique brand of outrageous humor. She couldn't believe this "filth" was allowed to go over the airways. A couple of days afterwards, she listened to and, unfortunately for Howard, taped Howard's now famous Christmas show which featured such innocent entertainment as a guy playing the piano with his erect penis, a gay choir singing "I'm dreaming of some light torture, some bruises just to make me moan . . . Masturbate. Humiliate." Then Howard commented, while watching two women spank each other, "The black lesbian is out of her mind with lust."

Apparently, this line crossed the line. Infinity was fined $6,000 — $2,000 for each station that aired the show (WXRK in New York, WYSP in Philadelphia, and WJFK in Washington, D.C.).

In a brilliant, typically Howard maneuver, he invited Ms. Stommel onto his local TV show for a debate, adding credibility by having Mr. Dick Cavett serve as moderator. But to no one's surprise, except possibly Anne Stommel, Howard came out dressed in a black bra and donning a big, black vibrator. Needless to say, Ms. Stommel was not amused, though I'm sure the viewers were.

The Christmas show wasn't the only infraction over the years that the FCC was concerned with. They cited specific complaints filed by individuals such as Anne Stommel and Donald Wildmon, and also listed several samples of Howard's antics that they say violate FCC standards.

They say that the Stern show has included frequent "lewd and vulgar" references in his broadcasts. The FCC defines indecency as "langauge or material that depicts or describes, in terms patently offensive as measured by contemporary community standards for the broadcast medium, sexual or excretory activities or organs."

Furthermore, they say that the Stern show "dwelled on sexual matters, including sexual intercourse, orgasm, masturbation, lesbianism, homosexuality, breasts, nudity, and male and female genitalia."

Anyway, some examples of the more controversial moments on Howard's show, taken totally out of context, might include:

* Howard had a graphic discussion about rectal bleeding.

* He had a conversation about Santa Claus fondling children.

* He talked about castrating and raping Mark and Brian, his two Los Angeles competitors.

* Howard also tastefully said he wanted to

defecate on the Hollywood Walk of Fame star monument of another L.A. radio competitor.

* Upset at the warm reception Paul Reubens (Pee-Wee Herman) received when he appeared on stage on a music awards show (after having recently been arrested for indecent exposure in a Florida porn theater), Howard said he thought that Reubens should ejaculate on the audience "and really give it to them right in the face."

* During a game called "Musical Crotches," Howard told one female contestant to "spread your legs and take your top off."

* Discussing the upcoming appearance of Cher on "Late Night with David Leterman," Howard hoped that Cher would appear in a sexy, skimpy outfit, and that she would defecate on the show.

If you're like me, you laugh just recalling the moments when Howard did all this stuff. Sure, some of it is raunchy, outrageous, and of a sexual nature—but all of it is funny.

* * *

As reported in *USA Today,* Ken Barnes, the editor of Radio and Records, said, "I think Howard is the biggest target they've (FCC) ever had." Mel Karmazin, President of Infinity Broadcasting, believes the FCC may not be too happy about Howard's on-air attacks. It's sort of a Catch-22 situation. Howard blasts the FCC for persecuting him, then they increase their attack in response to his heated defense. Of course, even if he didn't lambast the commission the charges would still be there. So at least we fans can enjoy Howard's venting his anger on the air.

Whether it's a wise move or not, Howard certainly doesn't go out of his way to make friends with the committee members serving on the FCC. In fact, when he learned that the then chairman of the FCC, Alfred Sikes, was being treated for prostate cancer, Howard startlingly piped in, "I pray for his death."

It's comments like those that push some listeners over the edge. "Now Howard has gone too far!" some say. And I have to admit, at times, I am one of them. I love Howard, and admire his impartiality when it comes to targets. But there are times when he does seem to be just cruel and not funny. In all fairness, though, that is the exception rather than the rule. And I even tend to doubt that Howard meant to be as mean as he sounded on the radio.

* * *

For example, the other day he was complaining about John Silbert, the President of Boston University (where Howard attended college), whom he claims is a "hypocritical douche wad." I'm sure Howard has his own reasons for hating the guy, but then he goes on to make fun of the man's deformed arm. At which point, his tirade suddenly stops being funny . . . at least to me. Of course, it's all a matter of personal taste.

The real point, however, is that Howard should have the right to say whatever he wants, as long as it isn't "legally" obscene, on the air. He is absolutely correct when he sees this as a First Amendment issue.

Over the years, however, Howard has certainly developed more enemies than friends concerning this FCC business. According to a December 1992 *Washington Post* piece, the infamous Senator Jesse Helms (R-NC), who sponsored congressaional efforts to impose a decency standard on the FCC, also had informally objected to Infinity Broadcasting's purchase of additional radio stations largely because of Howard Stern's program. He did eventually withdraw his letter of objection, however.

Meanwhile, the Southern California office of the American Civil Liberties Union leaped to

Howard's defense with this statement: "Howard Stern's rude social commentary and scatalogical humor are well within traditional First Amendment protection . . . and are hardly likely to harm children, who so frequently engage in similar humor themselves."

Mel Karmazin, according to *Newsday,* writes that Howard's contract "specifically provides for his termination without severance for his failure to observe the company's policy prohibiting the broadcast of obscene or indecent programming." And apparently there is a list of offensive words, which if said on the air, would result in Stern's firing.

When Howard held a rally for thousands of his fans at New York's Dag Hammarskjöld Plaza, protesting his being "crucified by the FCC," one of his guests was the colorful Grampa Al Lewis of "The Munsters" fame. Not quite understanding the spirit of the rally, Grampa Al, when asked by Howard to say something to the crowd, looked at the throngs of Stern fans and said the now immortal line, "Fuck the FCC!" Howard and the crowd went wild.

Meantime, Howard keeps on doing what he does best, maybe a bit more mindful of the bleep button, but for the most part, still throwing caution, and occasionally noxious fumes, to the wind. Hey, if the FCC can't take a joke. . . .

Ten

Howard's Kids

One time on the radio program Howard got a call from a kid who said he was a paraplegic. According to *New York* magazine, Howard told the kid, "No, from now on you're into sitting." He then invited the kid down to the station so that Howard could do a faith healing on the boy. "We had a great time. I even got him to apply for handicapped license plates for me. It tickled him that someone could be jealous of him. Then I got one hundred letters saying I was horrible. But the kid wrote and said it was the first time anyone kidded him and treated him as a real human being."

Our tendency is to treat handicapped people differently. Whether it is with pity or excessive compassion or alienation or even being too kind. Somehow we mostly can't get beyond their handicap. But Howard, to his immense credit, cuts through the crap. He truly does treat everyone the same — with humorous disrespect and disdain. Yes, sometimes, as previously mentioned, he does cross over the line. But now that I think of it, it is really my own inhibition about the handicapped that made me want to protect them against Howard's merciless barbs. Maybe they don't want my, or anyone else's protection. Like this kid, having his impairment made light of by Howard made him feel, well, normal.

Steady listeners are quite familiar with Howard's unique cavalcade. There was the woman with Tourette Syndrome, Quinton the Stutterer (Stuttering John doesn't really belong in this category), the woman with no arms and legs who played "The Star-Spangled Banner" with her tongue on "Howard Stern's U.S. Open Sores," and probably the most popular, Fred the Elephant Boy. Just to name a few.

Howard laughs at them, makes fun of them, embarrasses them — just like he would with any guest. He even found a hot date for Fred the Elephant boy. Something for which Fred is eternally grateful.

Fred had a minor form of palsy since childhood, which affects only his speech. He claims he used to stutter worse than Stuttering John. Now, unless he's very nervous, which doesn't seem to be too often, he hardly ever stutters. He got his nickname from Howard after Fred Norris played the sequence from *The Elephant Man*, where the title character says "I'm not an animal."

Fred enjoys the hijinks, and is not sensitive at all to the fun they have with him. He even critiques them. "Fred Norris can't do me, but Billy West does me real well."

In a phone interview, he recalled his first appearance on Howard's radio show. "About two weeks before the famous Christmas show they had the Tourette Syndrome Girl on for Dial-A-Date. So a friend of mine got the idea to call Gary and told him about me.

"Gary then called me up to make sure I was legit. Then the next day Howard called and invited me onto his show for that coming Friday. He wanted to check me out first to see if there was good material, and obviously he liked what he heard. He must have seen comedy when he heard me talk."

So he agreed to come on for Dial-A-Date. "As I said, I'm not a nervous type of fellow. But I did terrible on the radio. Even my mother said so. 'I've never been so embarrassed in my life,' she told me. She really laid the guilt trip on me."

The date itself, Fred says, was just okay. "She didn't know what she got herself into. After the date we went our separate ways. Afterwards, when I went back on Howard's show I didn't feel like talking about it. It's not my nature to talk about what happened. She and I just didn't connect."

But Howard wasn't about to let it end there. "So Howard gets me another Dial-A-Date, and this one was a go-go dancer in New Jersey," Fred recalled with some excitement. "She was a good dancer. There was one small problem, though. She took me home, and her boyfriend was there. So I just sat on the sofa. It wasn't really a date. I was more like the chaperone. But I always try to make the best of things. So I saw her at work and had a great time at a place I wouldn't normally go to. I'm not the type of person that frequents that type of establishment."

So how come she even called in for a date when she already had a boyfriend? "She just wanted to meet Howard, I guess. She was one of the strippers at that famous Christmas Show party, which by the way was like a Fellini movie where anything can happen."

To digress briefly, Howard does a special Christmas show each year. Fred recalled the one he attended as beginning "with two gay guys and a lesbian singing Christmas carols. Some of it was even too raunchy for Howard. This is the show where the guy played the piano with his penis, which got Howard into some trouble. But that guy was a bit wacko. There was also Rachel the Spanker who offered to give me a foot massage. It was great. She is a legit professional masseuse and dancer at night."

Anyway, now we move to a later Dial-A-Date. This is the one where Fred loses his virginity. "After the second date, I felt I had to make up a story, because I didn't want to seem like a two-time loser. So me and date number two made up stories about our escapades. She said I was a wild lover and some other bullshit. We did this for Howard. I didn't want to disappoint Howard a second time. And he believed us!

"Later I made a mistake when I was with the brat pack. I think it was Captain Jenks. [Captain Jenks is a diehard Howard caller who has been known to make prank calls on other radio and television shows.] I told him the truth about what happened that night, and Jenks must have told Shirley the typist. She came on the air with this info, and Howard asked me about it. I tried to bullshit that *she* was bullshitting, but I'm not such a good liar. At first Howard was disappointed, but later I think he understood my predicament.

"After that phone call I thought I was completely off the show. But soon after I did a favor for Howard. Someone was giving him some kind of award, and he wanted to refuse it the way that Indian woman refused it for Marlon Brando. So I dressed up like an Indian and refused the award for Howard. I did this just to get back on good terms with him."

Another time, Fred went out on a Dial-A-Date with a woman Gary had met at Howard's Super Bowl party. "She also had a boyfriend. . . . We had dinner with Gary serving as chaperone. She was very late, so I was eating alone for most of the meal, although she had called to say she would be late. When she arrived she was dressed up like a Contessa. She had a hat draped over her face and looked like she could have been in Billy Joel's video 'Uptown Girl.'

"So we go up to her friend's apartment. I wasn't nervous. I was very calm and collected because I didn't want her to tell Howard I was nervous. There was champagne on ice and romantic music. Then she slipped into the bathroom while I got myself ready. She then came out in something from Victoria's Secret. Very sexy!

"I was a virgin up to this point. I didn't drink much because I wanted to have full use of my faculties. But honestly I wasn't that nervous. I'm only a social drinker anyway. I never got drunk in my life. So, we made love, and it was good. It was wonderful. I think I saw so many movies, thank God, because I knew exactly what to do. It was just the way I imagined it to be.

"Afterwards, she smoked a cigarette, and then went into the bedroom and changed into another sexy outfit. Then we did it a second time. I was there until 3:00 in the morning. For the rest of that week I didn't touch myself even once. (He laughs.)

"When I took her home, every time we stopped at a red light she would make out with me. It was like having a girlfriend for a night. She really delivered."

It sure is easy to understand Fred's loyalty to Howard.

* * *

Like the rest of Howard's fans, I am anxious to know what Howard and the rest of the crew are really like. In that respect I'm sure we are all envious of Fred. He knows them all, perhaps not intimately, but certainly better than any of us.

"Everyone on the show is nice to me. Howard treats me like a regular guy. He is a great guy off the air, but he is very different. On the air, whatever comes into his mind he says. He doesn't hold back at all. Off the air, during commercials, he is less hostile and much friendlier. He doesn't talk to me too much during the commercials because he likes to save the material for when we're on the air.

"Robin and the others talk to me as well, and are pretty friendly. John is probably the least friendly. It's not that he's unfriendly, exactly, but he's got more of an attitude than the others. It doesn't bother me, though, because that's just the way he is. It doesn't really surprise me. He did cop an attitude with me, but as long as he's that way with everyone else then it's okay.

"We get along. We even went to Cleveland together because someone was holding a rally there to get Howard's sponsors off the show. John wore the same clothes the whole time we were there. He never changed.

"Jackie is always saying he doesn't understand what I am saying, but I know he's not really making fun of me. There are people who get a much worse ribbing than me. Besides, if they can zing it to me, I can zing it to them. I always have a sense of humor about it. They all really treat me pretty decent.

"I've also been on the television show numerous times. I think part of why Howard likes me is because I'm loyal and not after anything. I'm not like Celeste [the club-footed woman who seduces younger men.] I don't make phony calls like Captain Jenks. I'm just myself. I don't put on any act, and I don't make any demands. It doesn't bother me at all that I get paid just a little for some of the public appearances I do, because I do them just for the fun of it.

"One good thing about Howard is that he really opened me up. I'm much more outgoing now. I even have a social life. Before Howard, I never useed to hang out with girls. Now I do. So it was definitely worth it, going on his show. Now I'm trying to make up for lost time. I've also become much more of a tough guy since meeting Howard."

Did Fred ask to be in Howard's upcoming movie, *The Adventures of Fartman?* "No. If Howard wants me to be in it I would be most happy to do it, but I would never ask Howard to be in it. I'm not there to further my career, I just want to help out if I can. It they want me in his *Fartman* movie for just one second to say 'P.U.,' I'll do it. I did get to be ring announcer at a WCW match at the Meadowlands, though. It was great."

Eleven
TV Days

As long as I've been listening to Howard, he has been complaining about being stuck in radio, the armpit of show business. He doesn't care that he is the biggest star in radio, since he views television and movies as the only way to get the respect he deserves.

As a radio devotee, I don't quite agree with Howard, but I understand where he is coming from. He wants the limelight that comes with the visual medium.

Howard's desperation came through loud and clear during the Bill Boggs TV show. So when he finally got his chance to have his own show, he dove at the chance.

First, there was the Fox network. In spite of

Howard's "tantrum" on "The Late Night Show" with Arsenio Hall, Fox decided to give Howard his own show. Howard and Robin and the gang taped five shows, which according to Howard weren't as off the wall as he would have liked. The people at Fox had their own ideas and, as usually is the case, they differed from Howard's. In essence they handcuffed his creativity, not allowing the real Howard to shine through. It makes you wonder why they wanted him in the first place.

In any event, Fox cancelled the remaining shows even before any of these five aired. In fact, none of them ever did air, and I would give a lot to get a glimpse at them.

Naturally, Howard was pissed, and, as is his nature, expressed those sentiments on the radio, where he now seemed destined to serve out his entertainment sentence.

Then Channel 9 TV, a super station which broadcasts out of Secaucus, New Jersey, came to the rescue. They basically decided to let Howard do whatever he wanted, within the constraints of TV regulations. And what Howard did, in essence, was to simply move his radio show in front of the cameras.

I remember the anticipation of seeing his first show, which he promoted constantly on his radio show. This was a major event for Howard

133

Stern fans, and we eagerly awaited this new chapter in television history. And so did the critics, who couldn't wait for Howard to fail.

Well, the first show was uneven to say the least. As Howard even said, it was the ugliest show on television. Putting Robin aside (and maybe Fred), Howard, Gary, Jackie, and John are the motliest-looking bunch of slobs on television. It's not what you would call pretty television. But then again, it wasn't meant to be.

The format was pretty much a free-for-all. There were some planned bits, but for the most part I think Howard and the rest couldn't get over that they finally made it to television. It was still an event, but the celebration would have to be put on hold for a while.

Over the following weeks the look of the show never changed (terrible lighting, which was Howard's biggest complaint), but Howard's level of confidence grew and therefore so did the level of the show. Once listeners got used to seeing these once faceless voices, the viewers began to get as comfortable with the program as they did. Now the only worry was the critics, who by and large panned the show.

There were some enlightened professionals who stayed with the show, and began to appreciate its uniqueness. Channel 9, for their part, also seemed willing to give Howard a lot of rope. It was a wise move on their part. Howard's show eventually gave them the highest ratings they ever experienced, even beating out "Saturday Night Live" during their competing half hour in New York. Howard was finally a hit in the medium he so craved to be in.

And as we all know by now, Howard brought a new dimension to television, bringing things down as low as they can go. It was truly some of the most unforgettable hours on TV.

There was a tribute to the breast, classic interviews from Stuttering John, Lesbian Dating Game (my personal favorite), the fight between Geraldo Rivera and Frank Stallone, those unbelievable spokesmodels (some incredibly sexy, some pure skank), the Kielbasa Queen, near nudity, Howard practically mooning the camera, Howard's irreverent, but dead-on, impression of Senator Ted Kennedy, massages, making out with Martha Quinn, the Sexorcist with Linda Blair, the Homeless Howiewood Squares, the Prostitute and Call Girl Family Feud—just to name a few choice bits.

If you've never seen the television show, well, it's a bit hard to describe. Picture Dante's *Inferno,* but not as bright. The production values were cheesy at best, but sometimes, and I know

Howard would disagree on this, they conveyed the proper mood and setting for some of their wild bits.

Here's what took place on just one particular show:

* Dr. Judy Kuriansky, a sex therapist, came on to show her video of a Japanese Fertility Festival, which Howard referred to as a Penis Parade.

* The gorgeous spokesmodel did a split for Howard during a Snapple commercial, then writhed sexily on a bed during a Dial-A-Mattress commercial. Howard knows what sells better than anyone.

* Then Howard hosted a game called "Name That Tuna," where a panel of judges had to guess which one out of the three lady contestants was *not* a lesbian. The judges were Robin (whose "mocha hush puppies have been exciting lesbians for a long time"), a big lesbian named Bruce, and a porno star. It was actually hard to figure out who was the hetero, but it didn't really matter. As Howard says, "Lesbians equal ratings!"

* Next up was the popular segment featuring Stuttering John and his nerve-wracking interviews. Here are a few more of John's victims and his haunting questions:

To Penny Marshall: "Do you think Howard Stern is single-handedly saving the planet?"

To an angry Chevy Chase: "Are you still wearing a toupee?" To which Chevy replied: "What does he want? Does he want me to put his dentist in a higher tax bracket?" John, understandably, just stood there looking confused. Howard after watching this said with glee, "I love making him (Chevy) miserable."

To Art Garfunkle: "Does Paul wear a toupee? Why wasn't it Garfunkle and Simon?"

To Liza Minnelli: "How come gay guys dig your mom so much?"

* The show concluded with a typically tasteless, but hilarious, takeoff on "Gilligan's Island," called "Gag-again's Island." With guest stars Bob Denver and Dawn Wells reprising their roles as Gilligan and Mary Ann, Howard

rounded out the cast in drag as Ginger with a hairy chest. Very appealing. Fred was the Professor and Jackie played Thurston Howell III with his fat gut hanging out. Their goal seemed to be making this ugliest show on television even uglier. The grossest moment came when Gary, dressed in a monkey outfit, was beseeched by Ginger to share his boogers with the rest of the survivors. It was a disgustingly funny moment, but I swear you could see Bob Denver thinking, "What the hell am I doing here?!!" The bit ends with the survivors deciding to eat the dead Skipper in *Night of the Living Dead* style.

It was an hour to remember. And there were many more, but then the impossible, or at least ridiculous, happened: The show was cancelled!

According to Channel 9, in spite of the high ratings, the show was having trouble getting sponsors, and therefore it was an economic decision to cancel the show. Howard's version is different. He says it was his decision not to continue with the show. He always bad-mouthed Channel 9 management because they didn't know how to run a TV station. He was upset with the production values and lack of cooperation. But the main reason is that Howard now wanted to concentrate on his movie career.

Not surprisingly, Howard's show took a lot of heat when it was on the air. All sorts of groups complained, and that pressure might have contributed to Channel 9's alleged lack of interest in the show. Kevin McMahon, the former coordinating producer of Howard's Channel 9 show, defended Howard in a *New York Times* article. "We had a lot of handicapped people on, and people always complained we were exploiting them." This probably stemmed from a segment on the show called "Handicapped Defeat the Clock," where a man in a wheelchair and a man with prosthetic legs ran an obstacle course. According to McMahon, "We portrayed them as individuals. Howard always said we put people on who other people didn't want to acknowledge." Howard may have been responsible for some uncomfortable viewing, but you have to admire his impartiality and his total disregard for television standards and limitations.

Then came cable TV's E!-Entertainment Network. In October of 1992, Howard held a press conference at New York's Plaza Hotel to announce that he would be doing a weekly half hour interview show on E!.

This was exciting news for Howard fans, who

happened to get the E! channel. But according to Howard this may not have amounted to too many people, since at the time it seemed to be the invisible channel. "I'm here to save E!," Howard claimed. "Nobody can find the damn channel. One minute I'm watching a one-on-one interview with Lindsay Wagner and, seconds later, the Oyster Bay High School cheerleaders are warming up."

When asked how far he'll push the limits on his new show, Howard said, "I will burp and fart and see if they cut it out. I don't anticipate any problems over censorship." According to *Electronic Media,* Howard then pointed at Lee Masters, the president and CEO of E!, and Frank Shea, vice president of programming, and said they are "the two guys who will be fired if anything goes wrong."

Howard didn't expect any problems in booking guests. "I'm not total scum," he admitted. "Some people will talk to me. I've never had a guest leave the (radio) show unhappy. That's a lie," he quickly amended.

But according to a *Los Angeles Times* article, there were at least a dozen publicists and managers who refused to book their clients on Howard's show. They claim that Howard's producers were aggressively going after big-name talent, but were having a hard time securing guests. Naturally, E! officials denied that report, and said they have had no problem lining up guests.

L.A. publicist Jim Dobson said flat out in the article, "We won't do the show. We've had experiences with some of our clients on his radio show. While it's good publicity, it's not a good experience. He'll introduce Tina Yothers as the has-been actress of Hollywood, for example. He's very degrading, especially to women."

NOW, the National Organization of Women, certainly feels that way. Tammy Bruce, the president of the L.A. chapter of NOW, was astounded that E! would hire Howard, who she feels promotes sexism and violence against women. NOW even threatened to stage a boycott of the network. But Lee Masters placated them, at least for the time being, by agreeing to produce some special programming about women. I can only assume that Howard won't be involved in those particular programs.

These days E! is much more of a force in television. And Howard's interview show airs Friday, Saturday, and Sunday at 10:00 P.M. Most of them are repeats, which is fine because it's easy to miss them the first time.

So far, some of Howard's guests have included Garry Shandling, James Brown, Joan Rivers, Donald Trump, Suzanne Vega, Dick Cavett, Willie Nelson, Zsa Zsa Gabor, Richard Marx, Jason Priestley, Geraldo Rivera, and Grace Slick.

The format is pretty simple. First of all, each show is just Howard and one guest. No one else from his radio show is involved on this show.

Anyway, Howard sits next to the guest and asks the kind of questions you'd imagine Howard would ask. Not atypically, Howard spends a good portion of each show talking about himself. Sometimes it's endearing, other times it's distracting. But that's Howard.

Someone who worked with Howard on several of these E! interviews, who chooses to remain anonymous here, says that Howard was a pleasure to work with. "I liked him before I met him and even more so afterwards. He's easy to work with, but I can see how some people would find him a bit difficult. We happened to click right off the bat. I found him to be a real professional, who knows exactly what he's doing. He prepares well in advance of the taping, and tends to make it easy for everyone on the job."

Twelve

Let's Go to the Video

Before he finally made the transition to the small screen, Howard was able to sneak in a couple of times through the back door. He has had a Pay-TV special and two video projects over the years which he brilliantly and incessantly marketed by himself.

I remember when, several years back, Howard announced on his radio program that he would be doing "The Howard Stern Lingerie and Underpants Party" on Pay-Per-View television. At this point in time, I had already seen Howard, either on Letterman or somewhere else, but I had no idea whatsoever what the rest of the crew looked like.

I was faced with the perfect opportunity to

143

see this radio legend and his until now faceless cronies on television. I couldn't wait. But I did. In fact, I procrastinated so long I forgot all about it.

Then one weekend I was visiting with friends and they asked if I would mind if we all went over to a neighbor's house to watch the Howard Stern special. I was ecstatic at both being saved from my lack of initiative and also realizing that procrastination can save me $30.

So it was with great expectation and a touch of nervousness that we proceeded over to Kenny's house to watch the festivities. I was nervous because having never seen Robin, Fred, Jackie, or Gary, I had, as we all do, conjured up certain images in my mind. I was afraid I might be disappointed.

And my fears proved to be mostly founded. None of them, especially Robin, looked anything like I pictured them. It's not that they looked better or worse, just vastly different. I found over the next several weeks that my feelings toward the radio show had changed because of these visual realizations. Eventually I got over it, but it was a rocky transition.

Anyway, let's talk about the show itself. Sorry Howard, but it was a major disappointment. I had never witnessed anything so unorganized on television before. Sure, it was initially exciting to see Howard prancing about with all these sexy babes in lingerie, but the excitement wore off real fast.

Even some of Howard's famous friends from his radio show looked sincerely uncomfortable being a part of this, I hate to say it, embarrassment. It was almost like they spent months promoting the damn show, then realized at the last minute that "Hey, maybe we better put something together here." I mean some of it was wild, but sadly very little was funny. There was a guy who set his genitals on fire, which was at least memorable. And there was a depressing segment where Howard gave a homeless man some money and prizes. It might sound like a generous act, but there was something about it that made it seem more of an intrusion than charity. Once the show ended I remember we all looked at one another to make sure we all thought it sucked. It was unanimous.

But a couple of years after that fiasco, Howard was on his show trying to sell a videotape of a recent appearance he made at the Nassau Coliseum, a huge sports and entertainment arena. This one was called "Howard

Stern's U.S. Open Sores." Now, call me a fool, but I was ready to give Howard a second chance. He deserved at least that. Once again, I forgot to buy it, but was fortunate enough to have a friend who borrowed it from another friend and never returned it. So he lent it to me, and *I* forgot to return it to him for a long while.

Eventually, I did watch it, and once again it was an unpleasant experience. It was a filmed account of Howard's sold-out show and it was Stern-mania to the max. But apparently this was a case of "you had to be there."

Not being there, and obviously not getting caught up in the magic of the moment, is not the way to fully experience Howard. This time out things were a little better planned out, but the humor was still, for the most part, absent.

Now I know this makes me sound like maybe I'm not such a huge Howard Stern fan after all, but I assure you that's not the case. I love Howard. I love his radio show, and I love his now defunct Channel 9 TV show. I like his E! show. But so far these first two non-radio ventures were not up to the high level of his radio show.

The "U.S. Open Sores" tape opened up with

a black woman who had no arms (and I believe no legs) being rolled out on a gurney. She then proceeded to play "The Star-Spangled Banner" on an organ with her tongue. Of course it's amazing and outrageous, but it's not fun to watch.

Another part of the video was Howard playing tennis. *BORING!!* This time out there was a bit more outrageousness in the sexy women department, which is probably what helped sell the tape in the first place. But overall, it was an unpleasant, unplanned mess.

So life went on again as normal, with me waking up to Howard on the radio, and always grinning or laughing in bed as I did so. Then one day I heard him mention that they were looking for listeners to come down to the radio station with ideas for Howard's next video project. No idea was out of bounds.

At the time, I only worked a couple of blocks from the Madison Avenue building where Howard does his broadcast. So I figured what the hell, I'll go down and see what's happening.

Lined up against the building were a wide assortment of Howard's crazy fans, offering their wild ideas to Stuttering John and a cameraman. It was fun to watch. In fact, though I was already late for work I couldn't tear myself away.

Most of the ideas I overheard involved butt bongoing or something to do with lesbians. You know, the usual.

I had to come up with something bizarre. After a couple of minutes of getting up the nerve, I walked to the back of the line. Talking in front of people makes me extremely nervous, and talking to a camera even more so. Before I knew what happened, it was my turn. Stuttering John was talking to me and suddenly the camera runs out of tape.

So I rapped with John for a couple of minutes. I asked him how it felt to be a celebrity himself these days. He said it was pretty cool. The cameraman came back, ready to go. And John with microphone in hand asked me what I'd like to see on Howard's next video project. Profusely sweating, and talking inordinately fast, I said, "Okay. So Howard gets Richard Simmons on the show, and he ties him up. Then me and Howard do a Siskel and Ebert type of thing where we trash all of Barbra Streisand movies in front of an hysterical Richard." John looked at me for a moment, then said, "That's pretty wild." Of course it wasn't as enticing as the sexual suggestions

148

coming John's way, but I thought it might just be different enough to appeal to Howard.

But my delusions of meeting Howard and starring with him in his next video were immediately shattered when the couple behind me told John they were willing to do some butt bongo for Howard right now. They were quickly escorted into the building, and I realized that I should have told Howard I'd be willing to butt bongo my sister's bare ass for his video. Of course, I don't have a sister, nor would I ever do that, but it might have opened up a dialogue and I might have been able to convince a friend to pose as my sister. But the point was moot. I missed my opportunity.

And as you know by now, all of this led to the inception of Howard's most recent video, "Howard Stern's Butt Bongo Fiesta." This time I decided that after all the effort I put into trying to be a part of this project, I would go out of my way to buy it. I mean I'd rather see some butt bongoing than Richard Simmons tied up in a chair anyway.

My wife surprised me with it as a gift, and I have to say I enjoyed this one a lot more than the previous ventures. The 3-D glasses and 3-D effects were a definite bonus, but overall there was just a better quality to the whole proceedings.

Of course, there was plenty of grossness, like Boy Gary dressed up as a gorilla eating baby excrement from a diaper. But there were plenty of topless babes and Jessica Hahn, virtually nude, looking better than ever. The stuff with "Guess the Jew" involving the KKK guy, Daniel Carver, was a turnoff and slowed everything down.

Howard created a video worthy of him, at least when compared to what came before it.

Thirteen

Tidbits

Yes, we already recalled some of the countless bits that we will always cherish. But this chapter consists of juicy morsels with no rhyme or reason which are pure Howard.

There are the impromptu moments on Howard's show, which can happen at any time, that keep us tuned in. There's his lambasting, in his own inimitable style, of various guests which sometimes makes their heads spin.

But Howard is about so much more than that. He's not nearly as one-dimensional as his detractors claim. Sex is undeniably a big part of Howard's repertoire, but it's not the only thing.

So in order to give a decent cross section of what takes place on Howard's show, here is a random sampling of conversations, quotes, and memorable moments from the Howard Stern show:

* As we all know, no one is safe from Howard's daily attacks. Not you, not me, and certainly not the Filipinos. At one time or another, Howard has said some disparaging remark against every ethnic and religous group, among others. And he has certainly taken his share of heat for said remarks. But as far as I know, he had never before been challenged to a duel—until his Filipino bit.

Apparently Howard made a few comments about the Filipinos, such as "I think they eat their young over there" and "The Philippines is a country where the fathers sell their daughters for sex."

Anyway, not too surprisingly, some Filipinos took exception to Howard's on-air comments. One of them, according to *USA Today,* even challenged Howard to a duel "any place in the world."

Rene Santa Cruz, a Filipino broadcaster, was so incensed by Stern's anti-Filipino remarks that he felt drastic measures were needed. This led to the duel challenge, which was supported by Cruz's employer, Radio Mindanao Network. They agreed to pay Cruz's expenses if Howard accepted the challenge, which Howard as of yet has not officially done.

In addition to the duel, a $65-million suit was filed against Howard by the New Jersey based Filipino-American Citizens group. They accused Howard of insulting the "entire Filipino race," and the $65 million represents $1 for each Filipino in the world.

Howard's response so far has been to say that he didn't mean *all* Filipinos eat their young.

* On June 11, 1992, one of Howard's many fans called into "The Today Show" and asked guest Ross Perot, then a Presidential candidate, if he "ever had the desire to mind meld with Howard Stern's penis?" This one stirred up quite a bit of controversy in the media over Howard's "irresponsible" callers who disrupt various programs.

* On an obviously slow news night this past May, New York's WABC-TV did a piece on Howard prompted by some legal ruling regarding the pending FCC fines. According to the report by Doug Johnson, a judge ruled that Infinity Broadcasting must now pay the FCC fine of $600,000. On Howard's show the next

day, he excitedly denounced Johnson's entire report. Howard claims that what really happened was that Howard's company and others, as well as the ACLU, went to court to try to prohibit the FCC from dictating what goes over the airways. They cited the FCC as restricting Freedom of Speech. But the judge, according to Howard, ruled that the FCC will be allowed to set fines. The $600,000 specific fine is still being appealed. The WABC news piece then shows Howard at a previous press conference discussing himself. "I'm very honest about what I'm thinking. I think the secret to the success of the show has been that I always just opened my mouth and blurted it out even at the point of being embarrassed, even at the point of not being politically correct. I just say whatever's on my mind. I'm not that calculated."

For the next two days after this piece aired, Howard spent much time criticizing the shoddy journalism and inaccuracies, as well as taking it out on Doug Johnson, who according to Howard "looks like he's one hundred years old. He's the opposite of Ponce de Leon. He discovered the Fountain of Old."

In the midst of all this, Howard veers off on a tirade about how awful his school years were. He had a psychology teacher who threatened to fail him because he never talked in class, even after he told her he was uptight about talking.

Howard then continued to mock every word coming out of Doug Johnson's mouth. Finally, he decides to get Doug Johnson on the phone. Doug said that if he did in fact say that Howard's parent company already paid the fine then he apologizes and he was wrong.

Howard also corrects Doug about the now famous incident where Howard was allegedly fired from WWDC for his post plane crash phone call. "When the Fourteenth Street bridge accident occurred, I said on the air that I ought to call them and ask if that will be a regular stop. That's all. Then a year after I had left to go to WNBC, they said they fired me for making tasteless comments about the plane crash. It's ludicrous."

* In a previous chapter I talked about Howard reacting to some bad comments Jerry Seinfeld allegedly made about Howard. On a recent show, Jerry came in to face the charges. Howard confronted him on the "amusing idiot" and "funny jerk" comments. Boldly, Jerry admitted to having said them, elaborating that he feels Howard is funny but cruel. There was some tension there, but it seemed to be in

155

good nature. Jerry also made one of his brilliant observations. He said that the beauty of Howard's show is that Howard can announce a great bit coming up, and you know that you have time to take a shower and shave, then turn the radio back on and you still wouldn't have missed the bit. That's the truth, and even Howard admitted it.

There are literally hundreds, maybe even thousands of such memorable moments. And after so many years, there is no evidence of the Law of Diminishing Returns. Howard defies all logic.

Although Howard suggests on his radio show that he turned down a cameo in the current hit comedy "Dave" because he feels he should make his film debut in his own "The Adventures of Fartman," Howard in fact appeared in a film several years back.

In 1986, a detective spoof titled "Ryder, PI" hit the theaters and marked Howard Stern's feature film debut. According to Karl Hosch, the film's producer, co-writer and co-director, Howard was a natural. Dave Hawthorne, who did the Morty Gandhi bits on Howard's radio show, was starring in the film and suggested to Hosch that Howard might do a cameo. Naturally, Hosch jumped at the chance, and for an amazingly low $1,000 got Howard to play Ben Wah (Howard named his own character), an out-of-control newsman.

Hosch remembers this shooting day vividly. "He came into the studio quiet as a church mouse and just looked around. Then we told him to sit behind the news desk and I asked him if he wanted to go over the script. He said no, so I said, 'Action,' and he just went ape-shit, improvising all over the place. He started ranting and raving. I mean we wanted him to be off-the-wall, but he just went crazy, which was great. We loved it.

"When his scenes were done Howard said, 'Is that it guys?' And he was off and I never saw him again." An editor who was working on "Ryder, PI" was also doing some editing on a Howard project and Howard asked to see some of "Ryder." According to Hosch, Howard's reaction was, "This is a real movie. My agent's going to kill me."

Perhaps Howard wasn't thrilled by his performance, which might explain his reluctance to mention this film, although he has on occasion made obscure references to it. In any event, "Ryder, PI" featuring a much shorter-haired, mustached Howard Stern, is available on home video, which should be of great interest to all us diehard Howard Stern fans.

Fourteen

So, You Want to Talk to Howard . . .

So you want to call the Howard Stern Show and get on the air with Howard? Well, you might as well quit your job right now, because this might take some time. Every now and then when a lucky caller does get through, we'll hear them say something like, "I can't believe I got through, I've been trying for a couple of years."

What you may not realize is that they have actually been trying for a couple of years nonstop. That's all they do is call Howard, with an occasional shower or food break.

Why do these people go through all of this? Well, just to be able to talk to the

King, of course. But the better question might be, why do these people go to so much trouble to call and then when they miraculously do get through, have absolutely nothing to say? It's one of life's great puzzles.

When I first started listening to Howard's radio show, I was pretty much appalled at the way he treated the callers. He would yell at them, belittle them, call them insulting names, or cruelly hang up on them. You can almost see the crushed look on their faces after their idol has treated them like dirt.

But over the years I have come to see things from Howard's perspective. He has a show to run, and he can't waste his time answering the inane greetings of callers, nor by talking about something that is only of interest to the caller.

And the amazing part is that all of these callers are supposedly diehard listeners and fans, so they should know what *not* to do.

Maybe it's just that once you get Howard on the line all common sense flies right out the window. Maybe. Of course, the other possibility is that Howard is right when he says that most of his listeners are big dopes.

Being a listener, I'd like to go with the former explanation.

I think it is just a case of temporary dopiness. But it needs to be stopped, and there is a cure. Following are certain guidelines any would-be caller must adhere to if they want to stay on the line with Howard longer than a nanosecond:

1. AS SOON AS SOMEONE ANSWERS THE PHONE TURN YOUR RADIO OFF. There is a strong possibility that if someone does answer your call, that someone could be Howard himself. And as any listener knows, Howard gets extremely annoyed when callers keep their radio volume up just so they can hear themselves on the seven-second time delayed transmission.

2. NEVER OPEN UP with "HEY HOWARD, DUDE! HOW'S IT GOING?" First of all, Howard is sick of the word "dude." Second of all, if you've been listening to the show you already know how he's doing, because that's all he talks about. Just assume Howard is doing fine. Don't feel like you're being impolite if you don't inquire into his health.

3. HAVE SOMETHING TO SAY. I know this sounds like an amazing concept, but it will actually get you in good standing with Howard. Don't call up just to hear Howard's melodious voice. That's what the radio is for. If you have nothing to say, Howard will hang up on you and you'll never feel the same again. Besides, if you piss him off too much he may not take any other callers, so you'd be ruining it for others as well. Don't be selfish, think of your fellow listeners.

4. TRY TO MAKE YOUR TOPIC, WELL, TOPICAL. Don't be like the Chris Farley character on "Saturday Night Live" and just bring up an old Howard bit and say, "Wasn't that funny?" The best bet would be to have something intelligent to contribute to whatever Howard and Robin are talking about at that moment. If they are already discussing something, chances are they'd be more likely to talk to you on the same subject.

5. DON'T TRY TO BUDDY UP TO HOWARD TOO MUCH. He already knows you love him. We all do. He doesn't need you to kiss his ass.

6. MAKE YOUR STORY SOUND REAL. Second of all, make it about somebody Howard's not crazy about. Any derogatory stories about Roseanne and Tom Arnold will at least get Howard's attention. Chances are he won't believe you to begin with, but if your story sounds halfway feasible he might at least give you good phone time.

7. DO NOT TALK WHILE HOWARD OR ROBIN ARE TALKING. This is a big one. Too many times callers make the mistake of thinking what they have to say is of more interest than what Howard and Robin have to say. Trust me, you're not more interesting. Howard will give you a chance to talk, but you must wait for him to pause in his ramblings before you jump into the void. The most successful callers are those whom Howard forgets are still on the line. After a five-minute tirade on something Howard will go, "Oh, are you still there?" and is pleasantly surprised and respectful when they are. If you play the game right you can stay on the line for a while.

8. LAUGH ONLY WHEN APPROPRIATE. Don't laugh unless Howard says something funny. I know that many of us think every word out of Howard's mouth is a comic gem. But sometimes he's actually talking seriously on a subject, and it's disconcerting to have a caller laugh during a serious discussion.

9. KNOW WHEN TO HANG UP. In other words, don't spoil a good thing. If you've just had a decent conversation with Howard, but you sense that he is now ready to move on, say goodbye and hang up. There's nothing worse than someone who can't let go, forcing Howard to hang up on them. Many good callers retroactively tarnish themselves and the good portion of the phone call by staying on past the welcome point.

10. DON'T TIE UP THE LINE. In fairness to other would-be callers, once you've had a successful phone call with Howard, don't call again for at least a couple of years. You don't want to push a good thing, and there's really no need to get greedy. If you're a hit with Howard, just consider yourself one of the fortunate few and spend the rest of your life bragging about it. People like Captain Jenks are special cases. If Howard wants to hear from you more fre-

quently, he'll let you know. Savor the call, then get on with your life.

11. SAY SOMETHING OUTRAGEOUS.
If you're a woman, tell Howard you're a lesbian, or that you love to be spanked, or that you're willing to take your clothes off just to meet him, or that you fantasize about him every night, or that you'll only have sex with guys named Howard because you idolize him so much, or that you want to have sex with him so bad your loins are burning with desire. Chances are he'll talk to you. Now, if you're a guy, just say the same exact stuff but say you're talking about your wife.

12. NEVER USE YOUR SPEAKER PHONE.
There is nothing more annoying in the world than talking to someone over their speaker phone. Howard hates them.

13. DON'T GIVE UP HOPE.
If you hang in there long enough, you're sure to get through to Howard one of these days. But after all that perseverance and persistence and angst, you don't want to blow it. So each time you call, be prepared. Keep this list with you, study it, memorize it, eat it if that will help you in some weird way. But if

you follow my guidelines, there's a chance you'll become Howard's favorite caller of all time. Think about it.

Fifteen

Howard Unbound

Well, there's not much more to say, and yet there is so much more. That's the thing about Howard. Much of what he is about, and the things he says and does, deals with the same subjects over and over. There's the FCC, there's his when-will-it-be-made Fartman movie, his small penis, his mother calling in to discuss his small penis, his hateful imitators, his low-life competitors, his wife, and Jessica Hahn.

Howard can really beat a subject into the ground. But though we may occasionally get tired of the subject, we never seem to tire of Howard. The same passion that fuels his anger also fuels our interest, and there seems to be an endless supply.

Howard Stern is a phenomenon, and his phenomenon status is a mystery to everyone who's not a fan. He's a long-haired, crude, self-absorbed, paranoid nut who loves to speak his mind. Those same attributes are what endear him to his millions of fans.

If Howard can be summed up in a nutshell, which is where he emanated from, I feel comfortable letting Dick Cavett do it. In a *Daily News* piece, Dick is quoted as saying, "People are victimized by authority all day long. All those things that annoy you . . . it's good to see somebody take them on. He's funny because he does things on the radio that people would like to do themselves. He doesn't get enough credit for how well he gauges himself. He knows just how outrageous to be, and he lets enough decency show through, like when he calls his mother. It's rather endearing."

Contrary to public belief, Howard is human. It's just not so great for ratings to show that side of himself. But occasionally Howard does reveal glimpses of his true nature, though it's usually when he's not on the radio. In a *Rolling Stone* article, Howard tried to explain what made him what he is today. And if you know all the bits about Ben Stern, his father, you'll be surprised to find out that it was dear old dad who greatly influenced him, albeit unintentionally.

"I've had the same concept since the beginning. I'd watch my dad commute, and when he was stuck in the car, he'd just sit and listen to CBS news. And I thought, 'Wouldn't it be great if he was laughing? If every once in awhile he heard a disc jockey say something funny, something that made him glad he was there?' Whenever I ran into bosses who tried telling me my kind of show wouldn't work, I always thought about that one miserable bastard on the parkway in his car. And I just knew if I could make him happy, then I'd be all the rage."

It's a good thing that young boy was persistent, because if he let himself get discouraged by all of the brick walls along the way, there wouldn't be the Howard Stern we've come to love today. So, ignore the critics, Howard. And just keep making us laugh.

FOR THE BEST OF THE WEST, SADDLE UP WITH PINNACLE AND JACK CUMMINGS . . .

DEAD MAN'S MEDAL   (664-0, $3.50/$4.50)

THE DESERTER TROOP   (715-9, $3.50/$4.50)

ESCAPE FROM YUMA   (697-7, $3.50/$4.50)

ONCE A LEGEND   (650-0, $3.50/$4.50)

REBELS WEST   (525-3, $3.50/$4.50)

THE ROUGH RIDER   (481-8, $3.50/$4.50)

THE SURROGATE GUN   (607-1, $3.50/$4.50)

TIGER BUTTE   (583-0, $3.50/$4.50)

Available wherever paperbacks are sold, or order direct from the Publisher. Send cover price plus 50¢ per copy for mailing and handling to Pinnacle Books, Dept. 796, 475 Park Avenue South, New York, N.Y. 10016. Residents of New York and Tennessee must include sales tax. DO NOT SEND CASH. For a free Zebra/ Pinnacle catalog please write to the above address.

WALK ALONG THE BRINK OF FURY:

THE EDGE SERIES

Westerns By GEORGE G. GILMAN